All Clenched Up and
Nearly Finished

Mick O'Reardon

Grosvenor House
Publishing Limited

This book is published by
Grosvenor House Publishing Ltd
Link House
140 The Broadway, Tolworth, Surrey, KT6 7HT.
www.grosvenorhousepublishing.co.uk

A CIP record for this book
is available from the British Library

ISBN 978-1-83975-685-6

DEDICATIONS

Many thanks to Maurice Holloway who introduced me to Paphos writers group who gave me so much encouragement to start writing this book. A special thanks to John Goodwin and Bob Barker authors themselves who gave me lots of encouragement and advice. Also Bridlington U3A writers group who also gave me useful tips also. Phyl my wife showing patience and support.

Acknowledgement

Thank you to Anne Harris an old client for the front cover photo she took of me shoeing her pony.

How it all started

First of all, let me just say that I never intended to become a farrier. The job I intended to do was to be a blacksmith making decorative fancy iron work. I was good at metal work at school and desperate to avoid my father's choice of following him into the armed forces. I had started to look for a career before I left school and saw an advert in the local paper for an apprentice blacksmith. Although the job was 20 miles from home, the distance didn't put me off. An interview appointment was arranged a day or so later. I went along to the interview clutching examples I had made from my school metal work class, fully intending to become a blacksmith. Derek Spence, my new boss-to-be, was so impressed with my metalwork that he offered me a job. He told me he did lots of wrought-iron work, repaired agricultural machinery and did steel fabrication work. He also mentioned that he did one or two horses...!

Starting from the beginning

I was born in my grandparents' house in a little picturesque village called Lastingham, on the southern end of the North York Moors. Lastingham, back in the 40s and 50s, was a very farming orientated village. My grandfather always kept bantams, hens and one or two geese, just like many other families in the village. He grew his own vegetables, had a dozen beehives and sold heather honey. Being a young lad, I often helped my granddad with his many jobs. He was a kind man who had many friends, especially in the farming community. He often helped other farmers with hay making or harvesting, sheep dipping or helping to move livestock from field to field. More often than not, I was helping too. Nowadays, health and safety might have something to say about a seven-year-old rounding up a load of bullocks. I was never asked to help him, I wanted to. It was not like work to me. Grandad made work fun, especially the hay making.

When I was about eight or nine years old, my father, who was in the RAF, appeared. I didn't know who this man was at first, but it became obvious to me in later years there had been one or two problems in the early stage of my parents' marriage. At the time, my dad was stationed at Rufford near York, and my mother, sister and I moved into RAF married quarters.

Living in married quarters felt a million miles away from Lastingham. Gone were the hens and bantams and helping my granddad cut the grass in the churchyard or hay making. Life felt like living in the fast lane. There seemed much more traffic compared to the little picturesque village I grew up in. Looking back now, there were fewer things for us kids to do. Life was just hanging around the streets. There was nowhere to build dens in the undergrowth or hollowed-out rotten tree trunks, nor to go fishing for trout in the beck. When we played cricket at Lastingham, it was not just us kids but adults as well. Those cricket matches often finished because of bad light, which often happened at 10 o'clock at night. Nothing like this happened living in married quarters. Then there were the many changes of school due to my father's postings. How I hated it. Well, that was until I met Mr Edwards, my metalwork teacher at my last school. Arthur Mellow Village College, Glinton, near Peterborough.

I had never done metalwork at the previous schools I went to. It was not until I was in my third year of secondary school that metalwork was one of the subjects, and I took to it like a duck to water. Mr Edwards was a teacher who must have been in his late fifties. He was a man who seemed to have all the time in the world and gave his students so much encouragement. My first metalwork class was where the whole class had to make something simple like a toast rack or a lamp stand. I could never in a million years imagine that one day it would appeal to me, well that was until I found out how good I was at it. Especially when A's started to appear on my end-of-term school reports.

I became interested in making decorative iron work while still at school, and Mr Edwards gave me so much encouragement. First, as I have mentioned, making whatever exercise he wanted the class to make together, but after a year or so, I was asking him if I could build my own aquarium and flower baskets, etcetera. I say make for myself, which was a lie, it was orders I had received to make money. Often on lunch breaks, I would be found in the metalwork classroom with Mr Edwards. I think he knew I had got a little money-making scheme in operation but he never questioned me about it. He gave me lots of advice and encouragement, which in turn got me more and more interested in blacksmithing. I even made a part for one of my friend's dad's old motorbike with his help. He was a man who used to tell us kids there is no such word as 'can't' anything is possible, and this was the time I reminded him of his own words. I had asked him was it possible to make half a carburettor for an old motor bike. The bike part was not manufactured anymore, they were obsolete.

Mr Edwards took one look and said, 'We can't make that, can we?'

'Well, sir, you all always told me there is no such word as can't, so we can,' I replied.

Then with a grin and a stare at me as if to say *you cheeky devil* said, 'You're right, let's have a go.'

With a little bit of trial and error between us, we got the part made, and the motorbike started.

So it was thanks to Mr Edwards' time and patience developing my interest in decorative wrought-iron work, which impressed Derek enough to give me a job.

This snowballed into shoeing horses, which gave me a good living for the next fifty-odd years.

I must admit, when Derek asked me at the interview if I was interested in doing the odd horse, I had to think what on earth did he mean? How did horses have anything to do with wrought-iron work? Then it dawned on me: why of course, blacksmiths shoe horses! Today we are known as farriers. I had never seen a horse being shod in my life then. I had helped my grandfather when I was younger to round up cattle or sheep on some of his farmer friends' farms but had never had anything to do with horses. On top of that, I had lived in RAF married quarters since I was nine, so farm animals and horses were definitely not on my radar. I never expected in my wildest dreams that I would fit horses with shoes for the rest of my working life. I was lucky I never had to look for work, work always looked for me for the next 52 years.

When Derek said one or two horses, I thought he meant one or two a month as opposed to one or two a day. Back in the early 60s, all the farm working horses had, apart from the one or two, died out due to agricultural machinery and tractors making farming easier. Riding for pleasure was only for the wealthier folk. Two or three years later, things were changing rapidly, and more folk from all walks of life were starting to ride for pleasure. Five years after starting work, I didn't have time to do decorative iron work. The horseshoeing had now become a full-time job, and I was then known as a farrier.

WORKING FOR DEREK

I left school at 16 in June 1964 to start my working life. The 20-mile journey never bothered me on my 175cc BSA Bantam motorbike I had bought two weeks earlier. Although I could have left school then aged 15, I had stayed on at school for an extra year more to please my dad and to take my O Levels, but as soon as the exams were over, I left before the summer break started. I saw no point in being there when my studies were over. In fact, if it was up to me at the time, I may well have left before taking my O Levels. At the time, my head was telling me that I was never going to leave school. It felt to me as if I had been attending for decades. After all, what I thought then was I didn't need qualifications to get the job, but nowadays anyone who wants to take up farriery needs a certain level of GCSE passes. Then at the end of a four-year four-month apprenticeship, all young farriers need to pass another examination to fully qualify to become a registered farrier. It is now against the law to practise farriery without the necessary qualifications.

Derek had to take the small family business on not long after he had finished his apprenticeship due to the sudden death of his father. That happened one day when they were shoeing a horse together. From what he told me, his father had fitted and nailed on the horse's shoes, then he picked his pipe up and said to his son, 'Clench up and finish it off, boy.' (Clenching up is where the nails come out at the side of the horse's hoof and are turned over to form a clench to hold the shoe on, then rasped smooth and tidy.)

He had one or two puffs on his pipe, then dropped dead with a heart attack. There was no warning, boom bang gone, and no illness, just dead at 48.

No one can ever imagine how hard it must have been for Derek to have to deal with the death of his father and having to carry on with the family business at such an early age. This all happened in 1962, and by the time I arrived, Derek had employed Phil Brown (we called him Charlie) to repair agricultural machinery and to do steel fabrication work, and from what I can gather, another young guy to do the blacksmithing work and learn the farrier side of the job. I understood he only lasted a few weeks.

Derek's forge was situated in a little Leicestershire village called Knossington. His clients were lots of farmers from the surrounding villages who would bring broken machinery and implements that need repairing. Some had orders for farm gates and cattle pens to be made. Other people came and wanted some decorative wrought-iron work made. Then there were the one or two horses! His premises were not huge but big enough to get farm tractors and lorry into his yard. The workshop also had a room right next to the forge furnace where horses were shod. The rest of the forge was where general blacksmithing, steel fabrication and repairs to farm machinery was done. Next to the work premises was Derek and his wife June's house with one or two outbuildings attached.

For the first couple of years of my apprenticeship, I made decorative wrought-iron garden gates and flower baskets, etcetera around the horseshoeing. Occasionally I helped Charlie. He was twenty-one, five years older than me and a year younger than Derek. The son of a farmer, he was the sort of guy who could repair or make anything no matter how difficult or complicated the job could be. Unfortunately for someone so young, his teeth went rotten at an early age. He had only just been fitted with his new dentures and was proud of his bright smile… well, that's until I arrived!

Like I say, now and then I went out with Charlie to help him repair farm machinery or to do welding repair jobs. He was also a guy who would swear whenever things didn't go right for him. He called it his Anglo-Saxon language. By Jove, he did just that when I was helping him to repair a farmer's worn-out steel fencing down either side of his drive to his farmhouse.

The farmer didn't want to spend money on new steel to replace the old, twisted railings. We had to straighten and weld the old bent bars back to the upright posts where his cows had rubbed and broken the old welds. One bar had sprung away from the post, and with all my strength, I managed to pull it into position while Charlie welded it to the upright post. It seemed like ages that I was pulling when I shouted, 'Have you got it? I can't hold on much longer!'

'Yes, I've f***ing got it, let the f***ker go.'

Twang. It hit Charlie straight in the chops, knocking him backwards, breaking his week-old dentures. He started shouting something about a few kings who didn't go to heaven and people who didn't know their fathers and another word that sounded like bullocks.

(That sentence is in code of what he actually said.) Also, he didn't seem to be smiling at me either. It could have been a lot worse, though; yes, it could have been me who got smacked in the teeth. I don't think he was swearing at me, though, but more about his welding.

Derek was a guy who always looked, and he probably was, deep in thought about jobs that needed doing. Some days he would instruct me to load the van with different size horseshoes, and I would ask, 'Where we going today?'

His answer was always the same. 'You will see when we get there.'

With me having no idea where we were going and Derek's mind on other business, I used to think wherever we are going, it was never this far. Often, he didn't get into much conversation so I just sat there admiring the countryside as we travelled. Then, without warning, the air would turn blue like Charlie had when I knocked his teeth out.

'What's up? What have I done this time?' I would say, thinking it was me who had done something wrong again.

'No, no, it's not you, f***ing bastard hell, f**k, f**k, f**k,' he would say.

'That's a relief it's not me, so what's wrong then?' I asked.

'We should have turned off 10 mile back and gone to so-and-so, f***ing bastard f**k, f**k, f**k. Bastard hell, that's made us really f***ing late,' he replied.

This routine didn't happen just the once; it was time after time. I asked him in the end, wouldn't it better to tell me where we were going so that I didn't have to listen to all the f**ks and bastards when he had forgotten to turn off for the right destination.

CHARLIE'S VAN

About a couple of months after starting work, Derek asked Charlie if we could use his Morris 1000 van to go on our horseshoeing round as the work van was on another job. In those days, Derek's car was a new mini-van which we used when shoeing horses and an old Bedford that was used when out on welding jobs on farms. Sometimes we went in the old motor on our rounds but mostly in Derek's mini. (Nowadays, with more equipment, a little mini-van wouldn't get half the kit farriers need in.) On this particular day, Derek's wife needed the mini, and Charlie had a welding job on a farm and would be going in the Bedford. So he very kindly let us use his Morris 1000 van.

That day, one of our calls was at a farm that resembled the 1920s. The place would have made the TV program *The Good Life* look modern. They kept six or seven cows, sheep, hens, geese, and rats and no tractor. Well, I thought, rats must be part of the livestock judging by how many ran past us while shoeing the farmer's old shire horse. Yes, this old horse was used for ploughing fields and any work other farms did with a tractor.

At the time, the weather had been rather unsettled with plenty of rain. So the fields were what I would describe as a quagmire, although the mud didn't bother the old horse work-wise but it was causing a few problems to the old nag's legs. The old workhorse had got itchy, infected, swollen legs. Pus was oozing out from the knee down. The most likely cause was the farmers had not washed the mud out of the shire's feathers (fur) after work. Mites get into the skin and can be very contagious.

The horse's condition gave us problems as it was reluctant to let us hold its hooves up for long. It was a case of doing a bit before it wanted to put its hoof down, and when it went down, it went with a slam right on Derek's foot. After what felt as if the job had gone on forever, we finally got all four shoes on. The other thing was, besides Derek having throbbing toes, we both stunk to high heaven. The oozing pus was ingrained in our clothes, and although I washed my hands often, it must have taken a day to rid them of the smelly horse's legs.

Also we gave Charlie a problem as his van stunk to high heaven when he got into it to go home at the end of the day. I think the aromas lingered from our clothes and tools even though we had unloaded our kit. Charlie used his van as his car, and on picking his then-girlfriend up later that evening, it caused him a problem. His lady friend couldn't stand the stink and was not comfortable that the horsey aromas might be engraved in her clothes. Her outfit would need washing once she got home and folk must be able to smell them. Early next morning before work, Charlie had given his van a deep clean and banned us from ever using it again.

Two or three years after stinking out Charlie's van, I found myself in a similar position, although not to the extent we caused Charlie. It was while at my mate Nick's one evening, his dad had asked me if I would trim their three ponies' hooves when I got time. That evening Nick and I were going to a darts match at Nick's local pub. With all my farrier kit in the back of my Morris 1000 van due to me using it at work, I thought it wouldn't take me long to trim the ponies' hooves before we went to the pub. Although I had clean knocking about clothes on, I thought trimming the ponies' hooves, I wouldn't get them dirty. After all, the weather was warm and dry at the time, and it was not as if they had come out of a muddy paddock. The first pony went without any problems, but the second pony had thrush in its frogs. (The frog is the soft rubbery like tissue in a horse's foot, and thrush is bacteria that can make the frog go all squelchy and can give off a foul, smelly discharge if left untreated.) After trimming its hooves and attending to the thrush, I sprayed the pony's frog with an anti-bacterial disinfectant. The trouble was this product is coloured purple, and as I pressed the canister plunger to spray, the pony decided to fidget. I sprayed my other hand instead, and purple spray doesn't wash off. So I went to the darts match not only with a purple hand but stinking of the pony's infected hooves embedded in my clothes. I had tried washing my hand countless times throughout that evening, trying to get rid of the stain. I felt some folk were giving me a wide berth, although no one said anything to me.

As I say, purple spray has to wear off your skin rather than wash off, which brings me to a story with a groom girl one Christmas Eve a few years later. This young lady, who I will call Jenny, was on her day off and had filled herself up on alcoholic beverages at her local pub at lunchtime. In the afternoon, she arrived at the stables where I was shoeing the horses in a merry mood and up for a bit of mischief. She had got a couple of canisters of hair tinting spray in hand. I knew Jenny was up to something but I didn't think it would involve me. With my head down, bent over, fitting a horse's shoe, she couldn't resist it. My hair had a blue streak down the middle of my head. When I looked up, I noticed no one had escaped her little bit of fun. A lad who I will call Alan, who also worked as a groom, looked like a punk rocker. He was a fair-haired lad and his head had turned blue and red; he looked more like a member of the Sex Pistols.

Alan shouted to me, 'Grab her, Mick.'

So I did, and he ran to my van as he knew I kept a can of purple spray on a shelf near the back doors. With the canister in his hand and a cheeky grin on his face, I thought, *Jenny's going to get her blonde locks sprayed purple*. By now, Jenny was wriggling, trying to escape but Alan got hold of her jumper and pulled it up to reveal she got nothing underneath. Yes, she ended up with two purple breasts. I don't know how she explained that to the boyfriend she was living with.

LODGINGS

One cold, freezing late November morning in 1964, I arrived at work on my motorbike with my hands and feet frozen. I was having difficulty undoing the zip of my leather motorcycling jacket with numb fingers after a 20-mile journey from home. (Motorbike gloves were not so good in the early 60s.) The first and obvious thing to do was to warm my hands up on the forge fire. An old farmer – well at about 50, he was old to me then – who had just called in with something or other that needed to be repaired, had other ideas.

'Get them hands in the cold-water trough,' he shouts.

There was a water trough to cool hot metal next to the forge and ice had formed on top during the cold night.

'I'm not doing that, it's freezing, anyway the water is still all ice,' I replied.

Not letting me warm my hands on the nice warm forge fire, he broke the ice with an iron bar and plunged my frozen hands into the freezing cold water. I was now using language that I had learnt off Charlie. What was this guy thinking of? Did he just want a good laugh at my expense?

'They will be as warm as toast in five minutes, and not only that, they will stay warm for the rest of the day,' he told me.

Of course I didn't believe him after telling him he probably didn't know who his father was several times, but he was right, he did know his father. I found that my hands did stay warm all day, and also hot aches never happened, not like when I warmed them up on the forge fire. So every cold day I would dunk my hands into freezing cold water before starting work. The thought of doing it is not nice but it was worth it not to suffer for the rest of the day. I found this procedure helped when I had to work out in the winter elements where there was no shelter when shoeing.

This first winter was certainly becoming a trial travelling the 20 miles to work on my motorbike. In the evenings when work finished, travelling home in the pitch dark on icy roads was not nice. At least on a morning it was getting light, and on the small country roads it was a lot easier to judge where the icy parts were. Back in those days, we always seemed to get plenty of snow, and the worst part of winter had not yet started, and gritting isn't what it is like today.

A couple of weeks after the incident with my frozen hands being forcibly dunked in icy water, Derek's mother, Freda, happened to be at the forge one morning when she saw me arrive at work, again numb from the cold. She there and then offered me lodgings at her house, which was only three miles from the forge. I thanked her but asked if I could think it over during the day. Different plusses and minuses kept going through my head. I could cope with the three miles, at least my hands and feet would not be quite at the frozen state when I arrived at work. That was the biggest plus; then I thought of the minuses. Will I be allowed to go out on a night, will I meet new mates and will I miss my old mates. During that day's work, I mulled things over in my head. Do I leave home or not? I thought, yes, I can, the three-mile motorbike ride would be cut to a few minutes, that plus outweighed all the minuses. I can still meet up with my old friends on weekends. I didn't go out much on weekday nights anyway, I was often too knackered after a hard day's work. On Saturdays, I need not go home until mid-morning when the temperature had risen. By the end of the day, I had made my mind up. I would take Freda up on her kind offer. That night I told my parents my boss's mother had offered me lodgings in her house after seeing me frozen when I arrived at work. The next morning, off I went to work with a rucksack full of spare clothes and got myself flitted into Freda's little three-bedroom semi-detached house. That was the day I left home for good. I was only sixteen and nine months and proud to say I made my own good luck through hard work. I think moving out of home and fending for myself set me up for the tougher obstacles life could throw at me.

The only drawback when lodging with the boss's mother is you could always be at work. Derek could always get hold of me with Freda on the phone, whereas while living with my parents, they had no phone in the house, like many other families in the early 60s. There again, I must not have minded too much because I lodged with her for over four years. After all she had treated me like her own son.

A few years later, she even arranged a party for my 21st birthday in the local village hall. She had rounded up all my mates without me knowing, my parents were now living eighty-odd miles away and, somehow, she got in touch with them, plus Derek and his wife, June, and most of my work colleagues. Groom girls from the stables where I shod horses had been informed. She had, I later found out, got one of my mates to take me to the pub to give time for everyone to assemble in the village hall. When we were into our second pint, he said something about a dance in the village hall (it was dances in the1960s not discos), so off we went to the dance, not knowing I would know every person. Freda had also organised all the food. I had noticed her preparing loads of food, but I hadn't taken much notice because she often had big cooking days. I just thought it was for her new deep freezer.

Yes, Freda never queried me what I got up to or where I went but, more often than not, I would tell her. Often it was Knossington Fox and Hounds pub to play five and threes dominos for a penny a knock. I found I could win money for the next night's beer. I soon cottoned on that one of the old guys who loved to play never counted up what dominos had gone. So I used to make a fuss to sit before his turn, especially when four were playing, and I just collected the pennies off him.

Yes, the Spence family were really good to me, I felt as if I was one of the family. I was really looked after. Freda always sent me to work with a pack up and even got up early to cook a breakfast for me. I often told her I could do my own, but no, she insisted plus having a dinner when I returned in the evening. Sometimes she cooked for some of the gentry if they were having a dinner party, and it meant her not being at home when I finished work, so she would organise me to have my evening meal with Derek and June.

Another thing which I didn't appreciate then was what it must have cost the Spence family to train me up to be a farrier. I didn't at the time take into account how little I was paying for my lodgings. I would never have been able to afford to pay the proper going rate other places charged. I suppose it never entered my head the cost of all the different courses I was sent on to get me to where I am today. I did moan now and then, I was earning all this money and getting paid very little. It was only when I started working for myself did I realise I had not been treated that badly. I did on many occasions call Derek a prat behind his back when he got me to start a new job 10 minutes before knocking-off time. Well, I suppose a few years later I became a prat too when I got my own staff. I was saying the same to them as what Derek had said to me.

Yes, what it cost to train me up to be a farrier was quite a lot of money with all the courses that an apprentice farrier needs to attend. Perhaps I should have looked at not how many hours I worked, but how much work I put into those hours I did work. I often thought what I was being paid, I would have more than earned on a Monday morning. Derek must be raking it in, but, and very big but, which never entered my head at the time, I never thought about him having to pay me holiday pay. Then there was public liability insurance in case I lamed a horse, vehicle insurance which may have not being cheap with most of us under 25, college courses which lasted weeks and many unforeseen costs that a business incurs. Plus, Freda wasn't charging me the going rate for lodging in her home. Now I think perhaps it was me who owed a great debt to the Spence family to have got me to where I am today.

We could all have a laugh and joke with Derek. We could all give out what I call polite cheek to him and get the same back with no malice meant. I suppose we were lucky to have a boss who we could class as a mate. Although none of us called him a prat to his face.

DAYS NOT LONG ENOUGH

Working at Derek's some days never seemed long enough. None of us watched the clock. I remember going out with Charlie to do a repair on a combine harvester at around two thirty in the afternoon. We were so engrossed with what we had to do to fix it that time just seemed to fly by. It was only when the farmer's wife came out with some tea and sandwiches and said if we hadn't a home to go to, she had better feed us. Didn't we know what time it was?

'What time is it?' we asked.

'Eight o'clock,' she replied.

'Eight o'clock! We thought it must be nearer blooming five o'clock. Not blooming eight o'clock! God am I in f***ing trouble, I was supposed to pick the girlfriend up at seven!' shouted Charlie.

The problem with the combine was repaired, and Charlie knew he was in for a rollicking from his girlfriend, so he decided he might as well have a good rollicking rather than half of one and said to the farmer, 'Strike her up, see if it works.'

When the farmer struck the combine up, I never seen anything like it, when what looked like five thousand rotten hen eggs came shooting out of the back. It was like a machine gun spraying bullets everywhere, only these bullets were some of the best stink bombs I had ever come across. They splattered everywhere, with the farm now resembling the local sewerage works. Weeks later, the stench of rotten eggs was still there… The farmer had thought his hens had stopped laying.

Reg Ashton

Two years into my apprenticeship, Reg Ashton joined us only for a couple of months. He had had his own blacksmith and farriery business, but at 63 years old, he was swapping careers for a guest house in Bournemouth. At a loose end, he came to help out until the sale of the guest house was finalised. He had passed all his horsey clients on to Derek, who thought he would big help making the shoes for the horses and any general blacksmithing. I also got lots of valuable tuition off him on forge work on how to hold a hammer and where to place steel on the anvil. In fact he gave us all lessons and had good ideas on how best to go about work that was not straightforward not connected to blacksmithing.

I can remember a call to one of his old clients, who I will call Major Thorn, who had two horses to shoe. Reg knew the horses in question and said he would make the shoes ready. A big set and a little set. If the customer had said a big and little one it wouldn't have meant a thing to us. A big horse can have little feet and a small horse can have big feet, but with him knowing the horses it saved us time making a big variety to cover ourselves.

Two or three days later, we went off shoe the major's horses, and we arrived at the village not knowing exactly where the major lived. Derek asked a guy who looked as if he was a farmer worker if he could give us directions for Major Thorn's stables. It turned out the guy worked for the major but not with horses and said, 'Go to the end of the village, there is a field gate next to a phone box. Follow a track across a field until we come to a crew yard that has got two stables attached, and the horses are already stabled.'

So over this field we go and sure enough, there is a crew yard where we find two horses in the stables. A big one and a smaller one. No one was there but we carried on regardless with both horses standing perfectly; we had them shod in no time. Derek commented that Reg had not only made the shoes the right size but got the shape as well. They hardly needed altering to fit the horse's hooves.

Later that day, back at the forge, the phone rang. It's Major Thorn on the other end, wanting to know if we were still going to shoe his horses that day.

'We've been, your guy told us where the horses were stabled in the crew yard across the field, a big one and a little one,' answers Derek.

'Oh, them, they are not mine, I have let a friend stable his horses there. Mine are at home,' he mumbles.

We had shod the wrong horses, and I never found out what happened in the end but we never saw the two horses again. I don't even know if Derek got paid for them or not. We were certain that we had the right horses for how well the shoes Reg made had fitted.

SHOEING

Winter used to be the busiest time for horseshoeing. In 1964 when I started work, Derek's main horsey clients were hunting horses that were only shod in the autumn and winter months from the beginning of September until the end of April. When the hunting season was over, these horses were just turned out to grass for the summer months with no shoes on. Most didn't need shoes just to walk around grass fields, just a foot trim every six weeks or so. Gymkhanas were few and far between then, although they were on the increase so the odd ponies needed to be shod, although I suppose there was also one or two show jumpers. Not like today; horseshoeing is non-stop all the year round. I would say from about 1967 was when I started not to have time to do much wrought-iron work. The only work I was doing in the forge was making horseshoes.

The steel fabrication side of Derek's business, though, was really taking off from about 1966. He was making more and more farm gates and fencing, building big free-standing hay racks and animal feeding bays. With farms getting more modern and a lot getting away from the rickety old cow sheds and buildings, new purpose-built cattle barns were being built. In fact Derek made anything, and it was not only for farms but industry as well. He was also getting into a little bit of precision engineering. That side of the job was not for me, I was getting more and more interested in the farriery.

Derek decided Charlie needed more help so Mick Harrison joined the staff around August 1965. Now with two Micks, Mick H got called by his middle name, Steve. Steve, a year or so younger than me, was like Charlie who had good ideas for working out difficult and complicated jobs, and he too had lost his front teeth at an early age. (No, I was not responsible for him losing his teeth this time.) Thank God his swear words were very limited. Derek really wanted to do less horseshoeing and move his business into more of the making gates and railings, etcetera, for farmers' crew yards and purpose-built cattle barns. I had not actually started to shoe horses by myself, even though I did in Derek's presence. With Steve arriving, my trips out to help Charlie to do repairs on farm machinery and helping to erect farm gates and fencing was tailing off apart from some really big jobs where all four of us would go.

A year later, I was going on my own shoeing the horses. While Derek was getting more focused on the steel fabrication side of his business, I had started to organise my own days around the increasingly busy farriery work. I think he never did have a big interest in the farriery side, although he was very good at forge work. His interest was away from horseshoeing and was concentrating on the manufacture of cattle pens and farm gates and railing and any many other products that farms needed. It was the opposite for me, although I enjoyed the decorative iron work, the farrier side got me more and more interested. The only time I was involved in the fabrication work was if it was a slack day shoeing horses, and then sometimes I would deliver orders to the customers or collect materials from the steel stockist.

Around six months after Steve started, Charlie handed in his notice as he got offered another job. He hadn't fallen out with any of us. He felt he needed a change. So Steve seemed to get promoted to head of the fabrication and repair side of the workshop. I don't think at the time he knew that he was in charge, but if any farmer called with something that wanted fixing, they went straight to Steve. He just took over where Charlie left off. Although Derek was boss, I think he was pleased we all used our head when he was not about.

Steve, though, didn't have to be on his own long as Andy Hatfield joined the workforce. Andy had just left school, aged 15, and ended up working for Derek for the next 40 years. By now I was seeing less and less of my workmates apart from first thing in the morning or last thing in the afternoon.

MIKE SMITH

Michael Smith, who became Mike, was another newcomer when I was about three years into my apprenticeship. He was employed to help me to shoe the horses and do forge work. He had worked on farms before but never with horses, and like me, had never seen one shod before. I hadn't finished my apprenticeship then, but I suppose I became foreman of the farriery department and I was now teaching Mike. He was of medium build, and at least he had got all his teeth. He was also mega strong, didn't swear too much and was quite calm around the horses. Now he had started to help me, Derek's farrier days were getting less and less. His customers would often book with Mike and myself for the next six-week appointment before we left the previous one. Or if they phoned, often they asked when Mick and Mike could come to shoe their horses. They just took it for granted and got used to the idea it was just us two and not the boss. He didn't mind, no one was complaining, and after all, we were picking more work up and not losing any, and it gave him more time to concentrate on the steel fabrication side of his business.

Mike was one of the easiest guys I could have worked with. Neither of us worried about a difficult horse to shoe until we got to it. Getting hurt was not on our radar, we were young and indestructible. Derek was the more nervous one and often told us to leave and walk away from anything that looked dangerous. The owners could get another farrier to shoe them as far as he was concerned, but we had other ideas. No other farrier would want to come to a stable yard just for one wild horse and who would blame them. I certainly wouldn't. I would want the easier ones as well. For the sake of one difficult one, we would end up losing the whole yard which we didn't want. Both of us would sooner be out shoeing than stuck in the forge and were prepared to take the rough to get the smooth.

It was as if we were our own bosses. We were often deciding if there was time to shoe extra ones or time to nip into so-and-so to free more time up for the next day. Derek didn't care what we got up to work-wise as we were not losing work but gaining more.

DELIVERY DRIVER

By 1967/68, Derek's workforce had increased from three when I started in 1964 to ten. Believe it or not, two more Micks had joined the staff too. Mick Bottomly and Mick Grey. Mick Bottomly became Micky and Mick Grey to MG. Also Charlie had returned. Derek had also built a new bigger workshop at the bottom of his yard. It was installed with a big power saw, which cut through steel like butter. New welders and numerous pieces of state-of-the-art machinery which helped to cut manufacturing time in half. The old workshop stayed as the forge where I made my horseshoes and did general blacksmithing. The delivery truck had been swapped from an old Bedford van to a five-ton Ford Thames Trader lorry with orders getting bigger and heavier.

Some days I only saw my workmates first thing in the morning as I was out on the farrier round. Derek often asked me what I had organised farrier-wise. Would I be back in time to do a delivery to some far away destination? I remember one day in particular. An order of two farm harrows, which Derek's workforce had made that fitted on the back of a tractor, hydraulics had to be delivered to a firm in Leighton Buzzard. This was about a 150-mile round trip. Not getting back to the forge until two thirty in the afternoon, then a quick late lunch, I jumped in the lorry and left at about three.

Overtime sprung to mind that day with apprentice wages being not that good and any extra hours were all for the better. I made Leighton Buzzard in good time; I had to because the firm that ordered the farm harrows closed at six o'clock. Not knowing where in Leighton Buzzard this firm was, I needed to ask someone local for directions. Spotting a corner shop, I collared a guy coming out to ask which way I needed to go. I didn't need to get out of the lorry as it was a hot day and the passenger window was down, and he gave me directions through the open window. It turned out I was nearly in spitting distance but it meant turning around. With stopping near a side road, I checked in the lorry mirrors and reversed round the corner and went off to deliver my load.

Two days later a policeman arrived at the forge, wanting to speak to who was driving the lorry in Leighton Buzzard two days before. Also he wanted to see the lorry's logbook. (Tachographs had not been invented then.) Well, Derek's face went crimson because he knew, including himself, that we were all guilty of never filling it in when we stopped for rest or unloading and when we returned back to base. Whoever took the lorry out always meant well and made a start filling it in, but none of us seemed to get round to finish it when we returned. Anyway, on this occasion I had, to Derek's relief, and that page was shown to the copper, and he never took a second look at all that were left unfinished. The copper did have a bit of a grin on his face, and it turned out I had reversed over some guy's bike when I turned the lorry around.

'I didn't see no bike. Are you sure it was me?' I protested.

'Oh yes, it was you, but don't worry too much about it. He had laid it down half on the road, half on the pavement near your lorry's back wheels,' replied the copper.

'It must have been when I was asking for directions, I only stopped for seconds. Well, what pillock would want to park his bike under a lorry's back wheel; must be mental,' I said.

The policeman said he doubted if anything would come of it, it was just I had never reported it. I didn't know I had backed over a bike. Apparently, it had got caught under the lorry after I had reversed over it, it then fell off at the side of the road and, believe it or not, it was a bit bent.

Nervous horses

I think Derek used to know I got on better than him on nervous or unruly horses. He was always in a hurry, whereas I was not. The job finished when I finished, but with him having so much going on in his head, he always wanted the horse's shoes on 10 minutes sooner than later. He would shout and swear at it at the top of his voice. Insisting he was never going to shoe the blooming thing ever again. In those cases, it is better to stay calm, don't lose your temper. Shouting and raving can only agitate the horse even more, and you will probably get the shoes on 10 minutes quicker if you stay calm. That's not to say that some badly behaved horses do respond to a good telling off, but not one that is a bit on the nervous side. Time after time, I used to go to the same nervous horses by myself and fit the shoes without too much trouble. I used to talk more to the horse, let it know I was going to pick its leg up, give it reassuring pats. Whereas Derek used to dive straight in and yank the horse's leg up, or if the horse moved to stand more comfortably, World War Three would break out. I think I must have learnt to be calm with most animals through helping my grandfather when I was young. He never got flustered with any animal, and in a way, it rubbed off on me.

That is not to say I haven't had to square up a badly behaved horse and teach it some manners, but never a very sensitive one. I could usually tell by the first touch if the vibes were good or bad and how the animal was going to react.

I can remember one occasion when I was with Derek shoeing an old horse and a youngster. It was the first time the young horse was being shod and the idea was to tackle it together. We started the older one together, and while Derek was fitting the shoes, I picked the front foot up on the youngster, which was tied next to the older one. Nothing happened, it didn't try to pull back, rear or kick out at me. I thought I could be getting on with it instead of waiting until the older one was done. After all, he wanted the shoes on as quickly as possible. 'Time is money' was one of his many sayings.

Without too much trouble, I shod it by myself and I told my boss not to come near, the vibes were too good. I didn't want him near to upset the applecart. I knew what could happen if the youngster so much as moved when it shouldn't have done, he would very likely have blown his top. I suppose in another way I was lucky that I could say things like I did to my boss. Not to be nasty and very often he agreed with me about my ways. I did talk to the horses while I shod them, and I am sure he thought I was barmy when I started work. It was something he had never done, the only chatting he did was when he had lost his rag when the horse moved when it shouldn't have done. Well, it worked for me, and I am sure it helps and very often the animal understands too.

PARTYING

Mike and I not only became work colleagues but mates as well. After working together for a couple of years, we had got to know lots of girl grooms. One of these stables, run by an ex-army officer I will call Major Stevens, employed three girl grooms plus a housekeeper-cum-nanny. These girls had their own cottage on the major's estate to live in and told Mike and I that the major was going away on holiday so they were having a party in their cottage. Did we want to come? We were told some of their friends who were nurses would be there, girl grooms from another big stable yard would be coming too.

It didn't take us long, like point five of a second to say yes. Just us and all these nurses and girl grooms to ourselves. What could ever go wrong?

The party night arrived, and off we went expecting to be partying with loads of the opposite sex. When we arrived, what a shock, and we were soon brought back down to earth. All the girls were there with their boyfriends. Nothing was said about them all having boyfriends. They had all arrived at the party as couples. When someone we didn't know asked who I was with and I answered Mike, they thought we were a couple.

The other thing I was not comfortable with was the party had been switched from the groom's cottage into the major's mansion, seeing that he was away. It was the nanny's idea and with so many people there, I could see trouble happening. Mike said he was not comfortable either with the party in the major's home, so after about 20 minutes we both decided to leave. What a good move that was, things did get out of hand later on. Expensive carpets and antique furniture got stained, glasses and crockery got broken, and probably the worst thing of all, the major's whisky got watered down. Apparently, someone managed to take the tops off his whisky bottles without breaking the seals and emptying half the whisky out and then topping up with water.

A week after our 20-minute party, Derek's wife answered a phone call at the forge one afternoon. The person on the other end happened to be a policeman asking had he got the blacksmith's.

'Yes, can I help?' she answered.

'Would it be your husband who is the blacksmith?' they asked.

'Yes, he is. What's it about?'

'Well, it's him we want to talk to about a party the other Saturday night over at Major Stevens'. We have information he was there. We need to come over to speak to him.'

'No, not my husband, he does go out on Saturday but he goes to the White Lion at Oakham. Are you sure you have the right guy?' she pleads.

'Yes, the blacksmith, and this is the phone number we were given,' replied the policeman.

June exploded into a rage and came storming into the workshop all set to commit a murder on her husband. Mike and I were not there at the time, it's what our workmates told us later but the story went something like this.

'Derek, Saturday night, where were you?' she asks.

'White Lion. Why?'

'No you didn't go there. I will ask you one more time. Where did you go on Saturday?' she shouts hysterically with a face like thunder.

'White Lion, honest,' he replies.

Now all the other lads were listening with interest, thinking, *Where has he been, who's he been with? She's going to kill him.*

Then she shouts! 'You are a lying sod. I will tell you where you went. You were at a party over at Major Stevens'. I've just had the police on the phone about damage that happened in his house. They have your name and phone number. What on earth were you doing going there? I thought I could trust you.'

Derek is still pleading his innocence when one of the lads butted in and said, 'The other Saturday night, Mick and Mike said something about them going to a party. Are you sure it wasn't them?'

The other lads told us our boss didn't know if he wanted to be cross with us or relived that it might be us. His wife started to apologise for the commotion she caused when it looked like her husband was telling the truth after all. She wasn't going to divorce him. The police did interview Mike and myself and were satisfied with our story. The major still had us to shoe his horses, so it meant we both had a job, and Derek and his wife stayed married.

LECTURES ON DRIVING

Derek often spoke about us young ones meaning anyone younger than him, even though he himself was still in his mid-twenties. He would often give us lectures on driving his vehicles. He would say to us, 'When I was young lad, I used to drive fast, and you don't realise the dangers until you get older.'

It was only him and Charlie who had the accidents and this was his way of justifying his lectures. Well, if he had slowed down, he must have driven blooming fast 'when he was young lad' because my feet were often on the imaginary brake pedal in the passenger side well.

I remember on one occasion we were going down this little country road at breakneck speed when we met the weekly service bus. The bus filled the road, and with Derek going so fast, he hadn't time to brake. He swerved the van onto the grass verge to miss the bus, but this verge was a 45-degree bankside. All the tools and horseshoes were flying around the van like World War Two missiles, and how it stayed on its wheels I'll never know. Of course it was not his fault, it was the bus driver's!

Yes, he won the prize for the most accidents, with Charlie coming a close second. The rest of us hadn't had a crash but we still got regular lectures about driving fast, and the same phrase 'when I was a young lad'.

We often pointed out to him, it was him who has had the accidents not the rest of us. His answer was, 'Well, you can't drive until you have had an accident.'

One freezing cold early February morning, I nearly became a driver, according to my boss's saying. He wanted me to go to the steel stockist at Stamford. Sometimes it would be a lorry load of steel, but on this occasion, it was something small. Normally I would have gone in my own Morris 1000 van, but that particular day, it was having new brake shoes fitted. I was in for another lecture when Derek said I'd have to go in his three-year-old Jaguar car. I had heard his same words a thousand or more times:

'Don't crash it, don't drive fast, be careful, please.'

Me, being a cocky 19-year-old at the time replied, 'Course I won't crash it, I'm a good driver,' and off I set for Stamford.

Out of Oakham, a small town on the Rutland/ Leicester border, the road has a long straight bit. It was no effort for the Jag to register 100 miles an hour on the speedo. It was the first time I had driven a car at a ton. The old motors I had owned did well to reach 60 miles an hour, so I couldn't resist giving the Jag a bit of welly. I had heard reports Jags didn't perform too well in icy or snowy conditions but the main roads had been gritted so I saw no problem. I got to the steel stockist and showed my new wheels off to a guy I knew who worked there, trying to convince him it was my new car. No, he wasn't convinced!

On the way back with the radio and heater going, it was easy to not realise the temperature was dropping rapidly. The main roads were OK but not the untreated side roads. I was within two miles of the forge when a stupid idiot called Jack Frost had spread a load of ice across the road right on a double bend, and I hit it. The Jag went into a spin. My boss's lecture started echoing in my head. *Don't crash it, but never mind, if I do, I will become a proper driver!* The Jag hit the grass verge on one side of the road, then slewed around across the road to the grass verge on the other side, then back again. I don't know how many times this happened but I ended up facing the way I had just come from when I came to a halt. *Due to my good driving skills, phew*, I hadn't crashed it. (Damn, I can't drive yet.) The grass verges looked as if a farmer had used his tractor and plough on them, but there was not one scratch or dent on the car. Later that day, Derek went out, and on his return, he commented how the grass verge near Cold Overton was all ploughed up.

'What for?' one of the other lads asked.

'Well, some stupid idiot was going too fast and must have lost it on the ice; it's blooming icy on that road, you know,' he muttered.

'Yes, I saw that,' I stuttered, trying to look innocent and not telling them it was me that had done it.

Marriage

I met Judy my future wife in the summer of 1969 while she worked as a girl groom at stables where I shod the horses. She had lived in a cottage with other girl grooms but had decided that as her work was only seasonal, she wanted to look for a job that was more permanent when her contract ended the following spring. It was the time when I had left Freda's, and my new abode was at one of the other Micks, Micky Bottomly. Micky had got divorced about a year before after a short marriage and took me in as a lodger to help him out with his house rent. His home was in the village between Langham and Knossington called Cold Overton, and by God did it live up to its name in winter. One of the reasons I had moved into Micky's was because I was thinking of a career change but I didn't know when. Although I hadn't had any fallout with the Spence family, I would have felt it cheeky to carry on lodging with Freda, even though I had thought for god knows how long about a career change, I had never got around to doing anything about it. I met Judy about the same time Micky had met Margret (who became his second wife) and she was starting to spend lots of time at Mick's home. So after about six or seven months lodging with him, I felt it may be best to find a place with Judy.

So before Judy's contract finished in April 1970, we decided to look for somewhere we could make our home and 'live in sin' as it was classed then. We found a one-bedroom furnished flat in Ranksborough Hall in the village of Langham, near Oakham. I think the rent we paid was something like two pounds ten shillings a week (£2.50p). The flat consisted of a good size double bedroom, a large lounge-cum-kitchen and dining area, and a small bathroom. It felt as if both of us were not tied to house rules like at our other lodgings.

Ranksborough Hall flats all had lovely views. It didn't matter if your flat was on the front of the building or at the back. The rear rooms overlooked gardens and later a swimming pool, and at the front were open meadows. The only downside was we never told our parents that we lived in sin. If we were with Judy's family, it was her flat, and if we were with mine, it was my flat. As far as we know, it was only one of Judy's brothers and one sister and her husband (she had six siblings, I had four) who knew of our secret.

When Judy's contract with the stables ended, she had already found a job in an engineering factory. The work was nothing special but paid a lot more with less hours than at a busy stable yard. I think, at first, she thought it was wonderful to be working indoors on cold, wet days, but deep down, she missed the outdoor life.

About three months after she started work at the factory, Judy asked me had I thought any more about a change, work-wise. It must have been the best part of a year and a half had gone by with me thinking of looking for a career change since moving from lodging with Derek's mum. What I needed was someone to give me a shove to do something about it. Looking back now,

I know Derek didn't want me to leave, and I was not sure I wanted to because if the truth was known, I had only talked about leaving and done nothing about it. Well, that changed one night when Judy asked, 'Mick, do you know how to work a copy lathe.'

'Why?' I asked.

'There is a job going at our place. They tell me you could earn twice what you earn now.'

With our wedding getting near, and any extra money would mean we may be able to afford some sort of honeymoon. I heard myself say, 'Can you get me an interview?'

I was not certain I meant what I said, now it's come down to the nitty-gritty. I know doubling my wages would come in handy, but Derek trusted me to organise my own schedules. I never told my feelings to Judy but in the end, having more money won.

I got the job, which more than doubled the wages. Even though I didn't realise it at the time, working at Derek's was much happier and more rewarding than watching and waiting for some machine to finish. It was the most boring job I had ever done.

OK, there was a bit involved setting the thing up, but once that was done, you just stood back and let the machine take over. It would machine a bar of steel into whatever dimensions it was set up to do. Then a few minutes later you took the finished product out and put another bar of steel in.

At Derek's, I had been used to friendly banter, and soon I found the foreman or the foremen (there were plenty of them) at my new place of work hadn't got a sense of humour. I felt guilty for having to hang around waiting for the copy lathe to finish what it was doing.

If I saw anyone approaching, I would pretend to be looking to see if adjustments were needed when they didn't.

Other times, a time-and-motion guy would want to time how long a job took. Of course, it meant we both got time on our hands as the machine was not going to work any faster just because he was there. I often said to him he had a cushy job timing the workforce. Although my old boss didn't want us dawdling, he certainly didn't stand over me with a stopwatch expecting every horse I shod should take the same amount of time. To me this was a waste of time and money. In my eyes, the job finishes when it finishes. Not half done or corners cut, and I told this guy what I thought.

Of course he didn't agree and said, 'Firms need people like me for efficiency so the management know how to plan.'

Well if that was the case, they probably were not enough of them as the place went bust a few years later. The trouble was some of the managers, they hadn't got a clue how half the machinery worked.

For that matter, I was never quite sure who my boss was. Three guys would seem to organise different jobs for me to do and with one saying, 'Can you do this job? It's more important.'

How I saw them was, they just strutted around with a clipboard with sheets of notes attached. Were they the same notes as the day before? I don't know. I came to the conclusion perhaps they had passed a diploma in clipboards as they never seemed to be without one. They never seemed to look at notes attached to their clipboards as it was always wedged firmly under the armpit. Or were their white coats manufactured with them already attached?

Anyway, I would just get the lathe set up, and somebody else would want me to leave what I was doing and do something else that was even more important. I had probably wasted 10 minutes or so setting the thing up and have to start all over again to do another job. The management didn't communicate with each other and more time was lost faffing about through it.

I spent 24 years, well no, just under two actually, but it felt 24 boring years after watching time stand still in the engineering factory. As I have said, it was the most boring work I have ever done in my life. I used to think half an hour must have passed since when I looked at the clock last. Then got a shock to see the pointers had hardly moved. (That's another point, big clocks were dotted all around the factory floor. Derek didn't have one.) *Had the thing stopped?* I often thought, but no, it's just when doing monotonous work is when I found time must stand still.

I had come to the conclusion that I had made a wrong move leaving my old job. When I worked for Derek, I never once moaned about going in to work. I really enjoyed what I did and never worried what time of day I finished. I very rarely finished at five thirty the official knocking-off time. In fact most of the time I had no idea what time of day it was, and when I did ask someone, often it was later than I thought. I was used to hours not long enough, now they were too blooming long. Although the pay was better, I started to dread another day of clock watching. One way or another, I wanted to get back shoeing horses full time.

OUR WEDDING

It was 5 September 1970 when Judy and I got married. With money being short, we thought our honeymoon may be just a long weekend away. Going away to the exotic places newlyweds go nowadays was far from our dreams. At the time, we thought we were stretching our budget to a couple of nights at Skegness in some cheap bed and breakfast establishment.

Although I had left Derek's five months before our wedding, I still did a little farrier work in my spare time for extra cash. One of my clients, a farmer called Jim, who had one or two horses, mentioned while I shod his nags that he could do with some extra help with his haymaking. Did I know anybody?

'I do, when can I start?' I asked.

I ended up not just helping on weekends but two or three nights after work. I jumped at any chance to earn a little more. We really wanted a week's honeymoon and I didn't mind how hard I had to work to be able to afford it. Mind you, one day I thought Judy and I may have been able to afford to go to Barbados with the money I found in one of the haymaking fields. In 1970 not many folk walked around with a stack of £10 and £20-notes stuffed in their pockets, except for Jim. I was lucky to have had £3 on a good day apart from when I got my wages on payday. I had never seen a £20-note until I found this wad of cash. This money was scattered over a wide area in the field we were haymaking in, and I knew it was more than likely to belonging to Jim. He was a guy who, although very generous with his money, would sooner pay someone else to dirty their hands rather than his own. He liked to be seen as a gentleman farmer although he had got no big estate to look after. He would never lift a finger to help because his hands were always stuffed in his pockets but it didn't stop him supervising us guys. We often used to say, 'Look, Jim, can you clear off so we can crack on.'

Anyway when Jim pulled his hands out of his pocket, a load of banknotes must have fallen out too. It was late one afternoon when we had finished for the day. Jim had left five minutes before me when I spotted a £10-note, then another. As I gathered them up, I looked around and spotted more. I spent time following back in our tracks, and in no time, I got a handful of £5, £10, and £20-notes. It was into the hundreds. I had never held this amount of money in my life then. Although Barbados did flash through my mind, I did stop at Jim's farmhouse and ask if he'd lost any money, hoping he hadn't. Jim just put his hand in his pocket and pulled out more cash and thought it must be his as what he got looked a bit light to what he had started off with, and I am sure it was. The other farm workers I am sure never carried that amount of money. If I never noticed that first £10-note and spent time searching for the rest, I doubt he would have noticed he had lost it. So, with my honesty, Barbados had to wait, but we did manage a week in Ireland for our honeymoon.

Part time

As I say, I never actually stopped horseshoeing while working at the engineering works. I had got asked by several clients if I would still shoe their horse at weekends or on a night after a day's work at the factory. This first came about not long after Derek decided to pack up the farrier side of his business, which was not long after I left. I was a bit surprised that Mike gave up shoeing horses too but he must have enjoyed working for Derek as he too stayed there for the next 40-odd years, doing more welding work.

Anyway, back to me still shoeing horses came when the head groom at Major Stevens came to see me one Friday night. She asked if I would be interested in shoeing the major's horses, and that is when I first found out Derek had packed up farriery. Also could I shoe three that weekend? I knew the major had a small mobile forge and that was it. No motor or bellows to blow the fire up.

After a think, I heard myself saying, 'I will see what I can do tomorrow afternoon.'

First thing next morning (Saturday), I went to Pledgers, the steel stockists at Stamford to buy a few different sized bars of concave steel that horseshoes are made from. Boxes of number four, five and six in horse nail sizes, plus one or two tools I needed, although I had gathered a good selection over the years, and a medium-size anvil (that is now painted white as a garden decoration in my garden) on credit. I tied the bars of steel onto the roof rack of my Ford Anglia car and very steadily set off for the major's 15 miles away. On the way, I also called at a coal yard and bought a sack of small breeze (coke) for the forge. The journey seemed to take forever. My biggest worry besides damaging my car was if the police ever caught sight; I am sure they would have pulled me over for having an insecure load. The steel bars stuck right over the front and back of my car. Any little bump in the road didn't half make the bars of steel whop about.

I also had put our cylinder vacuum cleaner in the car, and I thought if I attach the hose onto the blow end instead of suck, it would work the same as bellows or an electric motor. After a bit of mackling with insulating tape and with the help of Ken, who looked after the farming for the major, we lit the forge fire and switched on the vacuum cleaner. I couldn't believe how well it worked and made three sets of shoes there and then, ready for the next day. It was more excitement and amazement at how good the forge heated the steel that I made shoes ready for ones that needed new footwear. The horses that needed shoeing were at some trials and wouldn't be home until later that night. The object of the exercise, though, was that Saturday afternoon was just to get the forge up and running ready for Sunday when I was expecting to make and fit the shoes all in one go.

Moving into our first council house

By April 1972, nineteen months after getting married, Chris our son had arrived in June 1971, and Judy was pregnant with our daughter Karen. We had moved out of Ranksborough Hall to the village of Manton between Oakham and Uppingham in May 1971. That house now overlooks Rutland Water. Unfortunately, when we lived there, the reservoir was being constructed. Our new home had a phone in but again with money in short supply, we couldn't afford to have it connected. Then out of the blue one night it rang. OK, it was somebody who had dialled a wrong number, and we realised we could get incoming calls but we couldn't ring out. That is when I started to give out my phone number. If we wanted to contact somebody, we went to the phone box. What surprised me was how quick my phone number got round in the horsey world.

Judy had often talked about me going full time on my own. I had collected a few more clients and made their horseshoes at the major's. Although the work I had picked up was a lot for part time, it was not near enough full time. Plus, I would need a proper workshop and money to kit it out. I had mixed feelings; yes, I would love to have my own business, but could I risk it?

But how I hated factory life. I started looking at other avenues.

As I have said, at the factory, life felt like it had lasted 24 boring years instead of two, when another farrier I knew, John Williams, asked me if I would like to work for him. I got to know John while working for Derek. From time to time, we would often meet through work in big livery stables. He also knew that while I worked in the factory. I never actually stopped shoeing horses and one Sunday morning, I met John and we had a chat.

When I left work at the factory on the Friday night, ready for the weekend, I never expected to be handing in my notice on the Monday morning. John had offered me a job.

Working back full time in farriery again was like paradise compared to factory life. I knew John could never match the wages of the factory, but the agreement was that I could still keep my Major Stevens and the other clients I had accumulated. This work would be in my own time, and I could make my horseshoes in his forge instead of a small makeshift forge at Major Stevens'. I could also buy steel and nails off him at cost price too.

Mr Bill Wiggington was John's old boss. He had worked for Bill for 12 years, but Bill was now at retirement age and gave him his business. Working on his own was starting to take its toll on him, plus his business was growing. Not only did he employ me, he took an apprentice called Mick Webster on too. Yes, another Michael.

John had worked for Bill since leaving school, and apart from shoeing horses, they did a bit of blacksmithing. Bill was a man we all admired. He was very patient, and anything he did he made it look easy. John was taught well, he in turn passed a lot of useful tips on to me. I have always had the attitude no matter how much you know, there is still plenty more to learn, and now I was learning more.

Working for John I found strange at first. Nothing to do with him but more how things were done. At Derek's, I had had my breakfast before I got to work. Now we would make horseshoes until nine thirty then stop for breakfast. Afterwards we would all go out shoeing. First, I didn't know if I liked the idea as it felt like having to work up a momentum after a break. At Derek's, I was used to snatching a sandwich when I felt hungry.

As time went by, I had my regular customers which John left me to look after. He supplied me with a van and left it to me how I did the day's work. John and Mick W would go out together mainly. Sometimes, usually on a Thursday, all three of us would meet up at a big stable yard together where there were lots of horses to shoe.

John, though, had one fault. Nothing to do with his farrier work because no one could ever complain about his work as he was a top farrier. Some days now and then he could be a moody sod, but I must stress it was just now and then. Most of the time we had friendly jokey banter between ourselves while we made horseshoes. However, when John had a strop on, I felt the atmosphere uncomfortable. How Mick W put up with him I will never know. I was lucky, I mostly only saw him for a couple of hours in the morning when the three of us made horseshoes for our day's work. All I can say, I was glad it was Mick who had to work with him, not me, when he was having a bad day. When arriving at work and had one foot in the forge, you knew if it was a good day or bad day as soon as Mick W or I said, 'Good morning.'

'What's good about it,' he would snap.

'OK, John, can you give us a clue what's on today?' we would ask, knowing he was in a mood by his body language.

'Use your head,' he would growl.

Nothing more would be said. We would make a set of horseshoes that was one of the most used sizes, and hope he came out of his mood sooner rather than later to give us a little hint what might be booked in that day.

It often worked if we said nothing, and all three of us worked in silence. He did tell us the day's work in the end, the silence must have been as bad for him as it was for us two. Those days the atmosphere was awful but thankfully were few and far between. Most of the time he was good fun and had a sense of humour.

The other thing that John didn't like was anybody to be better than him even though he set his own standards high. I found this out at a farrier competition where we had to trim and dress a horse's foot. Then make and fit the shoe and make a specimen surgical shoe of the judge's choice. This competition was the first for both of us and we would fire for each other. To fire is the one who is not competing gets the steel hot while the other is working on the horse or making the two shoes. It also involves wire-brushing the hot metal to get rid of any dirt or slack that is on the steel or holding a shoe in anvil tongs for the competitor to rasp or file. The actual making of the shoe, the fireman must not interfere with. There is also a time limit, something like 45 minutes.

The competition started with John competing halfway through the morning on the third round. After watching the first round, we both came to the same conclusion: even if we had a bad day, no way would we be last. I remarked to John how we could throw the horses' shoes onto their feet from the anvil better than one or two of the first efforts. Our confidence went from worried to one of us might have a chance.

In my eyes, John's attempt was really good, and by no means anything to be ashamed of. It is understandable to make little mistakes on your first attempt with a tight time schedule, in a hot and sweaty atmosphere and working as fast as you can go.

When the lunch break came, I used that time to make sure all my pritchels and stamps were sharp and perfect. Pritchels are like a small punch, to punch a nail hole through the hot steel when making the horseshoe. The stamp is like another type of punch but marks where the nail holes have to go. The pritchels, instead of having a round end, are drawn out straight and oblong. They don't taper to a point. If they are starting to get blunt through use, it will not punch a clean nail hole and time is spent cleaning the blur from the nail hole. It is important that the horse nail fits the nail hole perfectly, no movement from side to side and not too tight where the nail is forced through the hole. Then with my tools in tip-top condition, it was my turn.

The nerves were jangling, the adrenalin was flowing as my turn began. The worst time was waiting, and once started, my nerves seemed to disappear. The foot dressing went well and was judged while I was making the shoe to fit the horse. Sharpening the pritchels had paid off, and with one sharp whack with the hammer, I had a perfect nail hole and my confidence was on a high. It is also important that the fireman has the steel hot ready and wire-brushed ready for the competitor. There is no time for waiting, the last thing you want to happen is to run out of time. John was brilliant, hope I was for him too.

Time up and finished in time, and I was well pleased with my effort. When the judge has finished inspecting the work, all the farriers check each other's work. I have never heard a farrier telling another his work was terrible, I have heard them say when a job was brilliant. The vibes I was getting were really good about my effort.

The competition finished late afternoon, early evening. Thirty-odd farriers had produced high standards, and I was hoping mine was one of them. Now the nerves were jangling again, waiting for the judge to announce the results.

When waiting for those results, I didn't know then that was soon to be my first and last competition. When the judge announced the results, I found I was above John.

The following week back at work was when I discovered John didn't like someone to be better than him. Instead of being proud that I did well in the competition, it worked the opposite. While making my day's horseshoes, he picked a pair up I had made, 'grunted' and threw them across the forge, and said, 'How you beat me, I'll never know?'

Then spent an hour trying to make the most perfect pair of horseshoes, all nicely wire-brushed. Usually a pair takes 15 minutes, well it did if you wanted to make money. In competitions, yes, the horseshoes are all nicely wire bushed, that is to make the work look better, but not everyday work. When the horse has been ridden down the road for half an hour, you can't tell if they have been wire-brushed or not.

After that episode, I decided I wouldn't enter any more competitions, I didn't want to beat him again.

HORSE KICK

Having said that about John, it was only when he had mood swings when the atmosphere would be horrible. Most times he would be good fun both at work and social occasions. He was often concerned if a difficult horse was on my day's schedule, and he always said, 'For God's sake, be careful, don't get hurt, leave it if it's that bad and we will go back together.'

It was his attitude, no matter how much the owner was attached to the horse, it was no good to you if you were laid up for weeks seriously injured.

He used to tell me to be careful, although I think it must not have applied to him. One particular day, John and Mick W would fit a horse which was one I usually did.

'Don't turn your back on it or it will have you, kicks with both barrels (both back feet),' I told them.

'Oh, it was alright the last time I did it, good as gold,' John remarked.

Later that day, I arrived back at the forge and John and Mick W were already there. They both had started to make next day's shoes, and John was walking with a limp.

'Hurt your leg, John?' I asked.

'You were right. That bastard gave both barrels when I turned my back on it,' he replied.

He took the full blast of the kick on his backside, and the next day the bruise went from the small of his back down to just above the back of his knee. To his credit, he gritted his teeth, and he must have been in great pain and carried on the best he could. Every day both Mick and I would comment how much better he seemed to be limping.

FUSSY CLIENT

One of John's clients was a tall skinny woman I will call Edith Dyer. When Edith booked her horses in to be shod, she often forgot to say that she would need stud holes in the horses' shoes. The stud holes have a thread in, so a stud can be screwed in when show jumping or competing on slippery wet grass. If she didn't ask, we didn't put them in as there is an extra charge. She informed John that the last set of horseshoes she had difficulty screwing the studs in. When he told her, yes, it would be difficult as there was none in, she started bawling and shouting how she had told all three of us and we must listen in future. I heard her shouting only being a couple of stables away. Next breath, she is asking if we would like a cup of tea. John assumed she had gone off to make tea but didn't realise she came to lecture me too.

Although she was not shouting at me, I did hear John shout, 'If she comes to you, Mick, tell her to piss off.'

The look on her face was a picture, she stopped telling me off and asked if I would like a hot drink too. I think she knew she hadn't asked for stud holes, but it had to be our fault and not hers. Or if we put them in and charged extra that would be another commotion, insisting she never asked for them. Although I never did anything wrong and it didn't matter how well I shod her horses, she always had to inspect my work. I think it would have made her day if something was not up to scratch.

Evening shift

I worked for John during the day and evening and weekends for myself. Back then when I was younger, I would not think twice to start shoeing three or more horses after a day's work. On one of those occasions, I bumped into a farrier called Albert Woodford at a big livery stables. He was just finishing his day's work, and I was starting my evening shift.

'How many are doing now, Mick?' asked Albert.

'Three. How many have you done today, Albert?' I asked.

'I have shod six horses today,' he said proudly.

'Six? What you messing about; I manage that before breakfast, Albert,' I said, being a cocky 24-year-old with loads of energy.

Albert realised I was showing off how many horses I could shoe in a day, and six, plus having to make the shoes, was a good day's work then by yourself. Nowadays there is a good variety of readymade horseshoes that most farriers use, which makes the job easier.

'How old are you, Mick?' asked Albert.

'Twenty-four. Why?'

'Well I am 60. Wait till you hit 40, you will find yourself slowing down. When you hit 50, you slow down a lot more, at 60, the energy is nowhere near what it used to be,' Albert replied.

By God, have I remembered his words, did they come true. At 40, I had nowhere near the energy I had in my 20s, and by the time I hit 50, I knew what Albert was saying. At 60, if an owner had an unruly horse to shoe, I started to think it may be a good idea if its owner got a cocky 24-year-old with lots of energy to shoe it. I felt I was not up to those challenges anymore.

LAME HORSE

One of a farrier's nightmares is when a client rings to announce that their horse is lame after shoeing. Many things could have happened, sometimes nothing to do with the farrier, sometimes it is. The three most common farrier faults are nail bind or prick, excessive trimming of the foot, or too much sole pressure. A prick is when a nail enters the sensitive part of the horse's foot. This is more than likely to happen on a difficult, unruly horse or a horse with hooves not in good condition. The farrier listens to hammer sound when a shoe is nailed on. We have to make sure the nail is in the wall of the foot, a thin layer of non-sensitive tissue in the outer edge of the hoof. A dull thudding sound means it is going into the foot and if left, the horse goes lame. A nail bind is where the nail doesn't actually go into the sensitive part but presses on the sensitive part. Often after three or four days, the horse will come sound without taking the shoe off. Excessive paring and too much sole pressure is another cause of lameness.

Having said that, if the horse is difficult to shoe, it can become a different ball game. The times I have criticised other farriers work on a wild horse and thought what a rough job. I often changed my mind about the workmanship after I have had to shoe the same unruly animal. I often thought perhaps the guy who did the job last did well just to get the shoes on. Looking good was only a minor detail. Nailing the shoe on can be tricky if the horse is rearing or kicking and pulling you about. We listen to the sound when nailing on. If the hammering sound changes, it may mean the nail is going into the sensitive part of the foot, which we call a prick. We only have a thin wall that we can nail into. If the horse is rearing, pulling or kick every time the nail is tapped with the hammer, the farrier loses track of the sound. If a farrier does accidentally prick an unruly horse with hooves in bad condition, I could understand if he thought it was just plain awkward. This happened to me with one of John's clients, and he went into a rage, shouting at me it shouldn't happen if you're professional. I will argue that point because all farriers have at some time in their career accidentally pricked one while shoeing. The horse I pricked with a nail was a nightmare to shoe at the best of times.

It could kick, bite and rear from start to finish, and to make things more difficult, its hooves were not in the best condition. This made the nailing so much harder to get a nail in a solid bit of foot. Every time the nail is hit, the horse pulls or rears, trying to be as awkward as possible. I have heard farriers boast how they have never pricked a horse foot. I would call them a liar, or they haven't shod many wild bad-footed horses.

John told me the lady whose horse I pricked was going to have my guts for garters and she may not want me to touch her horse ever again. I told him it suits me, it's a cow to shoe.

Weeks later, he should have practised what he preached because the same thing happened to him. It was a Friday knocking-off time when he got a phone call to say a horse he shod was lame. He jumped in his van and off he shot to see what the problem was. Yes, it was an unruly horse, but John never said a word.

A few days later, I bumped into the owner who told me to tell John her horse was sound again.

'Sound? I didn't know it had been lame.' (I did really.)

'Oh yes, didn't he tell you? It's such an awkward sod to shoe, and he accidentally pricked it,' she replied.

I had also bumped into the lady whose horse I had caught with a nail, and it turned out she was not upset with me. Instead of being cross with me, she praised me up for the many times I shod her difficult horse and was happy for me to carry on doing her work. She understood that it was an accident. She said she was happy with my work and had told John she was not cross with me.

'It was a different story he told me. He told me you were going to have my guts for garters,' I informed her.

'Did he? I'll have a word with him. I want you to come for the next appointment, Mick,' she answered.

I wasn't going to say anything to John about bumping into the lady who supposing was going to have my guts for garters. Then when I found out he had lamed one too, I did have a word. I asked him why it was OK for him to catch a horse with a nail and not me. Again it was a case of 'if I want to tell you, I'll tell you'. I didn't ask anymore; I worked in silence and gave blunt yes or no answers when asked a question. I knew it put an atmosphere in the forge, but at least it put my point across.

The law of averages say it will happen from to time. There again, if a farrier is laming horses regularly, perhaps it is a good idea to look for another farrier.

John could probably have approached these mishaps in a better way than he did, in a way it was a bit of panic, which I reacted to and acted in the same way years later with one of my own staff.

Accident

A year after I started working for John, Judy, myself, our two children, and Judy's brother Ted plus Tinker our Jack Russell dog were involved in a road accident. Judy was driving our Vauxhall Viva van and entered a long bend when a speeding car came round the other way on our side of the road. She swerved the van towards a big wide verge, unfortunately a steep camber made the van turn over and over. The children, Karen aged one and Chris two years old, did not get injured. Luckily, they escaped the smash without one single bruise. This was due to me bolting two car seats into the back of the van, then fixing baby seats to them. Judy, Ted, Tinker and I were OK, although we did get one or two bruises. The van was a write-off, and afterwards I realised how lucky we were to have survived a mangled wreck. All one side of the motor was caved in. I had seen cars not so badly damaged in other accidents like ours and people have died. The car that caused it never stopped, but the young couple in the car following us did.

They took Judy and the children to the local hospital just to check that they were OK. Another motorist gave Ted and I a lift back home to get Ted's car. While at home, I rang John who had a Land Rover, and he said he would ask his next-door neighbour, a car dealer, if he could lend us his car trailer to get our wrecked van moved. We met John half an hour later at the crash site, only to find a policeman wanting to see my documents. He didn't seem to be interested in what happened but more if the van was insured and taxed. So, as the tax disc was not in the windscreen, we had to search around in the grass for it. (The tax disc not the windscreen as that was in thousands of pieces.) Of course, today, they would be able to tell in an instant on the police computers. Surprisingly with how badly damaged the van was and with the front wheels not in a straight line, I was able to reverse it onto the car trailer. Unfortunately the couple who were following us didn't have time to get the car's number. They were too busy concentrating on avoiding it too.

We followed John back to his place to help unload the wrecked van. This was the other side of John; when I was in trouble, he was there, and let me use his van that I used at work. He told me to let Judy drive it straight away before she had time to think about what had happened so as not to lose her nerve. Later that week I managed to sell the wreck to a guy who also had a Viva Van with a clapped-out engine. He knew mine had a brand-new engine when I bought it 12 months previously, and he wanted to change his motor engine for mine.

Skin problem

A couple of months after the accident, I started to get small, scaly, scabby skin in my scalp and on my elbows. Then the scaly skin turned into a thick crust. I had tried a variety of lotions and potions but the rash just kept getting worse. With the condition getting no better, I thought I may be feeding it with the wrong ointments. So after several tries at self-treating, Judy persuaded me I ought to seek medical advice, as my skin was becoming really uncomfortable and sore. I thought it must be something to do with my job, however when I went to the doctor, he told me it was nothing to do with my job; I had psoriasis. I had never heard of psoriasis then but it can affect just small areas on the body or the whole body. It is not contagious. The body starts producing new skin cells every two, three or four days instead of twenty-eight days, and that is why I got flaky skin. The shock of the accident had probably caused it, and once you have it, you are stuck with it for life. It does go away from time to time, but there are no set rules when or for how long. Sometimes it can stay away for weeks or months or even years, but any sufferers are on tenterhooks for it to return. Creams and ointments just help to relieve, they don't cure. It became a nuisance to me for the rest of my working life.

Socialising

While working for John, our social life was going to many dinner dances and balls and many other functions I never imagined I would ever attend. One function Judy and I had to attend was at one of John's client's, who I will call Sue Patterson, in her big mansion. Judy had helped out with her horses when Sue was stuck for a groom and both John and I used to shoe her horses.

Judy came home one day and said, 'I bet you can't guess where we have got an invite to a party.'

'No, you're joking; not Sue Patterson's. Hope she invites John and his wife.'

I couldn't believe it, the last time I was in a big mansion at a party I was not comfortable. That was at Major Steven's, the girl groom's 20-minute party. This time it was mixing with the gentry.

It was at that party loads of the guests who I knew from work kept congratulating me on the farrier work I had done for them. I must have worked for John by then for over three years, and Judy kept saying why didn't I go on my own, I could earn more money. It was after this one party I started to think it might be a good idea, especially when wealthy horsey people were praising me. I knew I had my weekend and night farriery, but it was nowhere near enough for full-time work.

Sue Patterson's party came and went and the thought of working for myself kept cropping up from time to time. The big fear was money because we had none to talk about. Also we had just moved from our two-bedroom Manton house in exchange for a three-bedroom at a village called Whissendine (another council house) and it didn't have a phone. If my part-time clients needed to get hold of me now, they got in touch with a neighbour and I would ring them back from the phone box. (God, how we are lost without our mobiles today.) With two young children, I had the safety of a regular income and extra from weekend work. Dare I take the chance?

Another year went by, and Judy and I had at odd times talked about taking the plunge but did nothing about it until we attended the grooms' dinner and dance night. That was the night my life changed for the rest of my working life. At the do, I got talking to another farrier called Andy Speck. He was thinking of leaving his farrier job at Dave Gulley's. Dave was a top rate farrier who Andy had done his apprenticeship with. He had been taught to a high standard and felt he wanted to move on to broaden his skills elsewhere. It was on this night he was telling me after a few drinks that he was going for an interview for another farrier job. The job was miles away and if the pay was not good or he didn't get the position, he was going to come and see me and we would work for ourselves. At the time I thought he had too much to drink and that gave him the idea. In the morning when he was sober, he might not remember what he had said, so I never gave it another thought.

Three or four days later, I had a phone call at work. It was late one afternoon when John's wife took the call in their house that joined the forge. There was a phone in the forge, but she usually answered the house phone to take bookings. Andy asked if it was possible to speak to me as I still wasn't on the phone at home. (We had just moved from Manton to Whissendine and were waiting for new phone lines to be erected due to our council house being new-build.) He was put on hold and she went to find me to take the call on the phone in the forge.

The first thing Andy said was, 'Hi, Mick, can I come round tonight to see you?'

'No problem, Andy, what time?'

I tried to keep the conversation to a minimum, as I had an idea we were being listened to on the house phone. I guessed why Andy was coming to see me, probably a little surprised that he meant what he said at the dinner dance. I had not even told my wife that he had spoken to me about us starting a business together, let alone my boss.

Andy came to see me that night near the end of March 1976, and we decided Monday 1 May 1976 we would start our business. He had already told Dave he would leave the last Friday in April (1976). I had a gentleman's agreement with John that if he wanted to get rid of me, it was one month's notice, and the same if I wanted to leave. The next day I thought it was only fair to tell him I was leaving as soon as I got into work!

Before I said a word to him, he said, 'Well, Mick, when are you leaving then?'

'Last Friday in April,' I replied.

That was that, no more was said until the beginning of the following week when I was told I was leaving end of that week. I was not a happy bunny being asked to leave two weeks early; for one, I couldn't afford a fortnight off with no money coming in. I would advise anyone now – if it's business, don't have a gentleman's agreement, get it in writing and signed by both parties, and both parties get a signed copy. If I had a signed copy of an agreement, I could have worked my notice out.

Working for John was not all bad, in fact it was a pleasure. Years later, that bitterness of getting rid of me earlier than I wanted probably had worked out to my advantage in the end. Some of his farrier skills had rubbed off on me to make me a better farrier, which I used all my working life. The fortnight I was not working, two blacksmiths were retiring and auctioneering their tools and steel off. With the limited amount of money between us, I bought a full-size forge, which I adapted so both of us could work from it, and a variety of concave steel that was for making horseshoes at one auction, plus an old Ford Anglia van for £35 at another. A gentleman farmer had given us the use of a big wooden derelict chicken hut to use as our forge. It's amazing how it never caught fire when shoemaking from the coke forge, and how it is still standing to this day. We thought it was ready for demolition in 1976.

With two weeks off, I had time to set it all up ready for Monday May 1st to change both of our lives. Derek's advice was, always look after number one, good advice: I did look after number one 'me' after that and got a good living out of it too.

In business, May 1976

Saturday 29 April 1976 was the day I started business unofficially with Andy in our first forge, a wooden chicken shack. That was to earn about £30 to start a business account at the bank on Monday 1 May officially. We assumed that while we were at the bank, we would ask for and get overdraft facilities. Nowadays, it is probably a lot easier to borrow money with credit cards, but in the 70s, we had to rely on the bank manager giving us a loan.

However, the bank manager didn't want to know as he refused us an overdraft. Our plan had gone wrong before we got started. Didn't this guy understand we were skint! Instead he lectured us for three-quarters of an hour on how we would not succeed in business and doubted that we would last three months. He said the main reason he couldn't give us an overdraft was that we had no collateral, which was true. I lived in a council house, Andy lived in digs on a farm, and neither of us had any savings. He also told us that surely there was not much call for shoeing horses in those days, and in his experience, we wouldn't make money.

We didn't know what to think at the time and one could say we were on a downer. I was worried how I was going to feed my family as we couldn't bank on a regular income then. We still had to build our business.

Andy looked at me and said, 'Sod him, Mick, let's show him. Course we can do it; we are not giving up yet,' with one or two extra words that started with an f and finished with ing to give more emphasis to the sentence.

I didn't know what to think at the time. I was still waiting for a telephone to be installed at home. Andy's lodgings did have a phone and his landlady didn't mind taking our bookings luckily. The old Ford Anglia van we bought for £35 (yes, when you saw it, one could see why it cost £35) needed new front tyres and attention to the corroded bodywork. Plus when the phone to our house was finally connected, it would have to be paid for. Advertising for work was out of the question then as farriery was classed as a profession and not a trade. (The rules have changed now where we can.) Yes, the bank manager had a point, but we would show him.

The lecture off the bank manager was probably what we needed. Andy had a friend who worked on a farm who was having a big barn-type building erected. He asked us if we were interested in painting all the RSJs (steel girders). We accepted even though the money was terrible it was better than no money. My old boss Derek asked if I was interested in making feet for gas fires he had orders for. I don't know how many feet I made but it was a lot, and it certainly helped the money situation. One of our clients (Andy knew him better than me) had a fleet of lorries and was often short of a driver so Andy would go. Anything that generated money, we did it. Oh and, of course, we shod horses in between.

Painting the van

One Saturday morning we thought we ought to try and spruce up our van. The idea was to fill in all the rusty spots on its bodywork. Gordon, the farmer who Andy lodged with, said we could use one of his farm sheds to work in. We spent the whole of one Saturday filling in holes with body filler and sanding it down and while we were at it, we switched the back wheels to the front and front to the back. The idea we thought was that the bald tyres wouldn't look so noticeable at the rear. Mind you the ones we swapped to the front were not much better. During the day, Gordon came to see how we were getting on. He also had a large can of green paint in his hand and asked if it was any use to us. It was some he had left over when he painted a fence a couple of years previously.

The following Saturday, armed with paint brushes, we set about making the van one colour instead of several from when we bought it. It didn't take us long before we had the old van looking brand new, although other folk may say otherwise. Both of us were hoping Gordon's paint meant for fences would be quick drying as we got a couple of horses to shoe that Saturday afternoon. At the time, we had to work when customers wanted us as we were still building up our business.

By one o'clock, the paint was still nowhere near dry so we had no choice but had to go with wet paint and hope no one would lean against the van while we shod the horses. We had not gone far when a policeman in his patrol car started to follow us. My first thought is he going to stop us. Yes, my first thought was right, he did.

Andy was leaping out of the passenger door before I brought the motor to a halt. He wanted to try to keep the copper's attention away from the bald tyres, and we certainly didn't want him covered in green paint. That could have given him the green light of an excuse to throw the book at us.

The first thing I got asked by the traffic cop was had I got my driving licence. He extracted his notebook out of his tunic pocket when I told him it was at home. Every time he went to write something in his notebook, Andy took his attention away by talking to him with anything that came into his head. The tactic seemed to be working and it was keeping the policeman away from the bald tyres and wet paint. I had an idea, seeing Andy was doing a good job talking the hind legs off a donkey to the policeman. Even though I had not got my driving licence on me, the MOT and insurance certificates were in the glove compartment. If I showed him them, he may be convinced the old van was legal. So when I got them out of the van and shut the door, I forgot not to touch the wet paint and got a green hand.

While the copper inspected my documents, Andy asked had we committed a road traffic offence, and what was the reason for stopping us, or was it my driving. He told us that it was a Saturday afternoon and we were in a hand-painted vehicle, road tax stuck in the windscreen with a bit of insulating tape. (I don't know how he knew our van was hand-painted!)

'I didn't know it was an offence to drive on a Saturday afternoon in a hand-painted vehicle with the road tax stuck in the windscreen with insulating tape,' I replied.

'It isn't,' he said.

'Well, what did you stop us for? We have just painted it, it is all we can afford, and we have just started out in business,' Andy replied.

'Oh really, and what business is that?' asks the policeman.

'Farriery,' we both replied, wondering what else he was going to ask.

'Farriers, you shoe horses? My girlfriend is getting a horse. What's your phone number.'

Not wanting to lose a customer, even though we could still end up with a fine, we did give him our contact details but we kept him talking about horseshoeing and horses. Anything that came into our heads. Even the sob story how the bank manager wouldn't give us an overdraught to start us off, so we ended up painting farmers' sheds to get by. In fact, we rattled on for a quarter of an hour.

We noticed he started to get fed up listening to us, as he kept looking at his watch several times, then said, 'Look, lads, I have just noticed the time. I must fly.' He jumped in his car and he was gone.

Andy looked at me and said, 'We bored him silly. You know what, I bet he will be telling his mates *don't stop that pair, they can talk the hind legs off a donkey*. He couldn't get away quick enough.'

'Well it worked, plus we gained a new client,' I chuntered.

The van tyres were finally changed after we squeezed another thousand more miles out of them. If the truth was known, the new tyres we got fitted were not roadworthy by today's standards or for that matter by 1970s either. I knew a car dealer who was selling cheap tyres with the markings scrubbed off that were meant to be fitted to off-road vehicles only. We thought they were better than what we had, and with the front ones now well past their sell-by date and the rear ones about down to the canvass, we splashed out and bought four. Fifteen thousand miles later, we did get rid of them too when we bought a new van.

When we turned up to shoe the policeman's now-wife's horse in the new motor, he thought it was a big improvement from the old Anglia van. I asked, in what way. He said when he stopped us, he had noticed all four tyres were illegal plus he noticed I got a green hand when I slammed the van door shut.

I couldn't help myself when I joked, 'Oh, was that all what was wrong with it.'

A NEW CLIENT

One night I got a call from a new client asking if we could shoe his daughters' ponies. He wanted to make an appointment for an afternoon when the girls would be home from school. I saw no problem and booked the appointment for 4.30pm. He went on to have a moan about his last farrier as his ponies were forever losing shoes not long after he shod them. He blamed the soggy ground in the field which the ponies were turned out in. The mud was sucking their shoes off. I thought, well, his last farrier may have a point as boggy ground can be the cause, but we needed work and accepted we may have the same problem.

The day came and what Andy and I were not expecting was the horses were still in the field when we arrived. Yes, if it was a summer's day that would be OK, but this was November. We thought the horses would be up at their home in stables not half a mile away. If it was just a foot trim, I think we would just about have had time before it became dark, but not two full sets of shoes to fit.

So I said, 'I thought you had stables with lights when you booked for late afternoon. It will be dark soon.'

His reply was, 'Don't you work in the dark?'

'Not really; we can't see too well,' I replied.

Not wanting to lose the work, we did go to the field and found the two girls waiting with their ponies.

Luckily there was a concrete standing by the gate, which was a plus as none of us guys like muddy fields to work in, full stop.

By the time we got the horses' hooves dressed, ready for fitting new shoes, yes it was pitch dark. So due to our old van's battery on its last legs, we started the engine and left it running while we shod the horses in front of the headlights. It was not at all ideal as with our heads down we were working in our own shadow. The job seemed to last forever.

When we finished, I said to Andy when we were driving away, 'Their dad had a right go about the last farrier always losing shoes. I am not surprised if these were the conditions he had to work in. I couldn't see a thing. I only knew if I got the horse's shoe a bit proud on the outside of its foot when I burnt my finger when feeling if it was proud or not when fitting.'

'Aye, I was the same. God knows what the job looked like. I couldn't see much either,' Andy replied.

Three months went by and we had started to think we were not up to scratch and had he had somebody else. Then one night I got a phone call, and a voice said, 'You did a good job on our ponies and they are way overdue. When can you come again?'

I thought this time if he wants his daughters to be there, I will make it a Saturday morning and we were not getting caught out again. We really thought that this client was not happy and found a new farrier as we not heard from him.

When we arrived on the appointed Saturday morning, it surprised us how well the ponies' shoes were still on. Usually after three months the old shoes have started to sink into the overgrown hooves and the clenches have risen. Not in this case, none of the clenches had risen and the shoes were not embedded in the ponies' feet. I thought perhaps we ought to shoe them all in the dark.

Work started to come thick and fast only three months or so after starting on our own. One or two folk thought we may be a bit green to business and tried to knock our price down. I can have a stubborn streak in me and had the attitude that if you do one person's work cheaper, you end up the same with everybody's. I have heard all the excuses why we should shoe horses cheaper. One was, so-and-so only charged me x amount.

'Why aren't you still using them?' I would answer.

'Oh, we were a friend of the family, or the shoes didn't last long,' were some of the usual answers I often heard.

And my answer to them was, 'I have no friends in business, and you get what you pay for.'

We both said we will stick to our guidelines and wouldn't budge with our farriery prices. It was the best way to avoid bankruptcy not having to do favours for so-called friends of family. Another thing I had learnt off Derek was don't undersell yourself. Whatever people think, it is you who has to make a living and having to work undercutting others is not a bright idea. Let your good work do the talking. I have seen where some businesses try to be too cheap, but to make a living need to cut too many corners just to survive. If they only started at the going rate, they would have had more time to do a decent job. Another thing is if you realise you want to raise your fees to the going rate through inflation, it will be a bigger hike than others. For example, if Joe Blogs charged £50 and the going rate was £60 but through inflation, the going rate went up to £65, and Joe Blogs wanted to be the same, his clients would have a £15 increase. Others would only have £5. I have found folk moan to others how prices have risen, but the Joe Blogs might be not so popular amongst their customers.

Saying that, Derek never undersold himself, and I can remember one day he told his clients that he had to have a price increase in 1964 from 25 shillings (£1.25p) to 28 shillings (£1.40p) for a full set of horseshoes. He was probably right from what materials had risen by and did he get plenty of stick. I was one who thought it may be a big hike as I only earnt £3 a week. Many protested you can't put it up by three shillings (15p), Derek. How times change; the going rate is around £75 to £80 as of 2020 to have a horse shod and inflation increases usually are at £5 a time.

The first guy to try this 'friend thing' on with us was a bloke I will call Fred Preston. Fred had two or three ponies that his kids competed on at shows. Both Andy and I knew him only because he was well known at the various horsey competitions he entered. Neither of us had ever socialised with him but as soon as we started doing work for him, the old pal act started. He would say how we were above the other farriers and what they were doing wrong, etcetera. When we finished shoeing his ponies, he was happy with our work and we were the best thing since sliced bread. That soon changed when he got the idea he was probably not one of our best mates when we gave him his bill. He found we were just like all the other farriers.

He wasn't at all pleased we were charging him the going rate and told us, 'You're joking, you're not charging me all that, are you? Mates see each other right.'

Then tried to confuse us, converting the price into the old pounds, shilling and pence money and what the cost was when he was a young lad 30 years ago. Decimalisation had been in force five years by then, we didn't want paying in the old money and anyway prices had risen. It ended up him telling us that never to set foot in his f***ing yard ever again. We were robbing bastards and will never get work with those prices.

One evening years later, I got a phone call from our so-called mate. He asked if I remembered him and was I interested in shoeing his show ponies again. By this time I had stopped taking on new clients and had people on a waiting list to get on my books.

My answer to him was, 'Why would I want to come into your yard when you had told me never to step foot in it again. Besides, you also told me we were robbing bastards... I don't want to rob you again.'

I never got so much as an 'I'm sorry; I was a twat for trying to belittle you,' so even if I could take a new customer, I wouldn't have done his ponies.

He asked, did he think Andy would come, did I have his phone number? I told him I can do better than that, he'd happened to call in to see me and was standing next to me, and he could talk to him right now. I said I couldn't answer for him. Andy mouthed to me, 'Who is it?' and I whispered back, 'Fred Preston.'

He curled his face up and didn't really want to talk to him but did, and he too said, 'No thanks.'

Another horse owner thought we may be a bit green and tried to get us to pay his vet's bill. One morning the postman delivered a registered letter to my home which had to be signed for. It was addressed to both Andy and me but Judy took delivery of it. At the time, we had just moved from the chicken shed to a bit better forge at Mountsorrel. Luckily, we just had a phone installed in the forge and Judy thought it looked important and rang us. She asked if she should open it. I told Andy, and with both of us wanting to know, she read it out to us.

It was from a guy whose horses we had shod seven weeks previously. His letter looked quite frightening, and he tried to be impressive using big, long words. I don't think he even knew what they meant. To cut a long story short, he was telling us we had lamed one of his horses when we had shod it and wanted us to pay his vet bill.

We knew which vets he used and we had always had a good working relationship with them. We had a good idea which horse it might have been, but after seven weeks we smelt a rat. A horse wouldn't wait seven weeks to go lame after it was shod. It would be lame the same day. We were both sure it wasn't our fault. We knew he had competed at some hunter trials a week after this horse got its new shoes. If the horse was as lame as he made out, no way would it have managed to compete.

This guy's stables were all ramshackle and not very clean. The horses stood on what looked like three foot of deep litter. (Deep litter is where the stables are not mucked out and new straw is placed on top of the old stuff.) The first time we entered his stable yard, we thought at the first glance the horses must be about 19 hands high. Their heads were nearly touching the stables ceilings, then we soon realised they were stood on a bed of deep muck.

The one horse we thought it might be was not well behaved and its hooves were not in the best condition, which made our job even harder. At the time, Chine House Vets had just two vets, John Craven and Michael Minns. We thought we would straight away get hold of them and found it was Michael who checked this horse out. He told us it was not us who had lamed the animal but how we managed to get shoes on that wild horse was unbelievable considering the setup. It turned out the horse had stood on a scrap bit of wood with nails sticking out in a rubbish-strewn paddock.

When we told Michael about the threatening letter we had received, he said he would have words with the guy as it was a dirty trick what he tried to do to us and he expected him to apologise to us. The owner did ring me later, and I told him we smelled a rat before we finished reading his letter. He would have to get up a lot earlier in the morning if he wanted to catch us out, and to let him know not to use big, long words in letters before he knows what they mean.

Apprentice

After about three or four months in business, we started to show signs that we could prove the lecturing bank manager wrong. Work was starting to come in thick and fast. I am very proud to say all our work was through recommendations, and that was the case all my working life. We didn't look for work, work looked for us. The only help we had was two clients (one I knew, one Andy knew) who had faith in us and lent us £50 each when they heard the bank had refused us an overdraft. Four months later, we paid them back, and we were able to triple our wages from £20 to £60 a week.

One year later, we got enough work to take on our first apprentice, a young man called Paul Skeels. We knew him from when he was one of our clients and still at school. He kept his horse on a small stable block on a farm with several other people who had horses. Paul often organised the other horses' shoeing appointments when their owners had work commitments or whatever and couldn't attend.

He had taken an interest in farriery and often hinted that when his exams were finished, he would work for us. He was a natural, his firm but calm ways made our job so much easier. It was just as well some of the other owners couldn't attend, because with him in charge we got their horses shod a lot easier without their owners.

Gradually, usually on Saturday mornings, Paul would turn up at our forge to help, and he was determined not just to hold horses while we shod them. He learnt very quickly how to make a decent set of horseshoes. By the time he left school, he was turning up every day, and we had started to take for granted that we expected him and we were giving him a wage.

Then one day, Andy said to me, 'You know what, Mick, we ought to get Paul signed up as an apprenticeship, he has been with us six months.'

So that's how he started working for us, we never asked him, and he never asked us either.

Paul was a guy who never complained about late finishing or early morning starts. He was a guy who never questioned how many hours he had worked, but how much work had gone into those hours. His interest with horses was not only shoeing them but competing at horse trials, show jumping and gymkhanas, etcetera. He was also good at schooling unruly horses and making them into good competition horses. They would then catch another horsey person's eye who would want to buy them. He used to buy and sell regularly. He often bought a horse cheap, often one that had got the boss of the owner. He would spend time schooling it, take it to various horsey competitions, do well, then sell it for three times what he paid for it. Very often, he would buy the same horse back again for a quarter what he sold it for. He would then spend time schooling it a second time, get discipline, take it to shows, then sell it for a second time. This next time probably four times what he paid for it? He wasn't a big guy but he was strong as an ox, certainly he used his strength but not in an aggressive manner.

OUR NEW FORGE

A year after the bank manager's lecture, we had moved from the wooden chicken hut to a solid brick building which became my forge for the next four years. The old Anglia van had got traded in for a brand spanking new Honda TN7 van, and we bought a six-year-old Morris 1000 van too. The telephone had been installed at home and one in our forge. All paid for.

The brick building, our new home, was better than the chicken hut but not exactly perfect. It came with problems soon after we moved in. Andy got offered it one weekend. The woman who owned it was all for us moving into it, as it would earn a bit extra revenue from an empty shed for her. At least this old building was not built of wood, but brick. It had no electricity and at our expense we didn't mind having it wired up to the mains by a qualified electrician.

After we moved in, our new landlady asked if we could shoe her two horses, which we thought would be extra revenue. It was not until we had shod them, she told us that it was the rent we agreed plus shoeing her two horses every six weeks. Letting us get moved in then telling us we had to shoe her horses for free was not on. We had only agreed a monthly rent, nothing was said about the horses. We didn't even know she had horses when we looked at the building. When we went to pay the rent for the second month, she had increased the rent yet again. The first month's was just to get us settled in, as she put it. It was something we were not expecting or agreed to. There was no choice but to pay it or move out. We felt we had got conned and she knew what she was doing. It was either stay put or move back into the chicken hut, and now with Paul starting working for us, that was not an option. The wooden chicken shed was not big enough, let alone it was a fire risk, so it was a case of biting the bullet and paying the inflated rent. Not only that, she wouldn't give us a rent book or contract. A year later, she had a bright idea of a nice stone wall she wanted built around the forge to partition it off from the edge of her field to make a little yard for us. We thought that would look nice until she told us it was to be built at our expense. I thought we will build a wall when I see pigs flying, so for three years she got fobbed off with different excuses why it didn't get built.

Psoriasis

Not long after Paul started working for us, things went a little wrong for me; I ended up looking like *The Singing Detective* covered head to toe in psoriasis. I had never had it this bad in the three years since it was first diagnosed. My body felt like it was dressed in rough sandpaper, with scaly skin covering all over my back, legs, face, hands, feet, arms, chest, and a thick crust in my hair. Four or five times a day I would rub ointment into my skin to take the soreness away. It was a case of gritting my teeth and getting on with it. For the last three years, I only had small patches on my elbows and a thick patch in my hair and more of a nuisance. This was the first time it had covered my whole body and was it uncomfortable.

I was leaving a trail of skin everywhere I went. Judy was trying to persuade me to take time off, and one Saturday morning I had to agree. My skin was so sore even smothered in ointment, and not only that, I could barely walk. Judy had watched me get out of bed, and I was trying to head for the bathroom to smother myself in greasy ointment. The trouble was I never made the bedroom door, never mind the bathroom. I just couldn't walk without help. I had to give in, but we had got a day's work booked in.

That Saturday we had got loads of horses to shoe at our forge. It was just as well we were working at the forge, as we had horseshoes to make before the first horses arrived. What the plan was all three of us were going to start making the first lot of shoes together ready for the first two or three horses, which would arrive together. When they arrived, one of us would carry on making horseshoes, and the other with Paul would start shoeing. We had arranged for two or three horses to arrive together at hour and a half intervals so no one was standing about.

Plan B had to be thought up quickly because we were at the limit for three; two would have had no chance. I wondered if BrIan Porter a friend of Andy and I would be able to help us out. He was a guy who never seemed to be in a hurry but got results quicker than other farriers working at a hundred miles an hour.

Judy rang Brian and told him my predicament and luckily for us he could help. Judy then phoned Andy to say I wouldn't be there, as I was in no fit state to get out of bed, never mind working, but Brian was coming to help. It didn't surprise Andy; he was surprised I managed to keep working as long as I had.

They did manage without me, Andy phoned later that Saturday afternoon to say that they had finished and how was I? She told him she called the doctor and he took one look at me and got me into hospital. I was in a room off one of the wards in Leicester General Hospital and little did I know then, but that was going to be my home for the next two months.

Psoriasis had never stopped me from working since diagnosed three years before. It had only attacked my elbows, knees, and in my hairline. It was more an unsightly nuisance and just a little sore before, but now it felt as if I had been rubbed down with rough sandpaper head to toe. It was so bad that I had to be pushed around in a wheelchair in hospital. It was even painful and a major operation getting to the en-suite bathroom in the corner of the room I was in. Skin was all over the floor, in the bed, on bedside cabinets, basically any surface I had touched or been near, there was dead skin. If I rubbed my feet or hands together, it felt like rubbing two pieces of rough sandpaper together.

The specialist who was treating me put me on a drug called methotrexate. This drug is used on cancer patients, where it slows cancer growths down. The idea here is to slow my skin producing new skin cells every day or so, the same as with cancer growths. One of the side effects is that it can give the liver a right bashing, so that meant loads of blood tests and really bad headaches. The specialist didn't think the headaches were anything to do with methotrexate, but the nurse told me not to take an aspirin in case the two didn't mix. The headaches came and went so I never mentioned them again, I just put up with them. Every three days, I was given ultraviolet light treatment, which was on the other side of the hospital. I felt so helpless having to wait for a hospital porter to push me there in a wheelchair.

After two weeks, I thought I was getting a little better. I told the porter I might try to walk back to my room. It usually took him five minutes to get me to the ultraviolet department, and I had all day to get back. He had different ideas, thank God. I did start the walk back when my ultraviolet session was finished, and after five minutes and no nearer my room, I was in trouble. I was walking like a kid who had pooed their pants. My skin was still thick with psoriasis, in fact it was still thick all over my body, not just my legs. Nurses kept asking me if I was alright, and I would smile back and say, 'Yes, I'm fine,' when it didn't take a brain surgeon to see I was not alright. Then they would walk off and leave me. I think they thought they were talking to Quasimodo with my stooping body and my scaly skin that made me look like a scary monster. Every step I took, it felt my skin on my knees was going to crack open and bleed. What the hell did I do now?

Then I heard a voice say! 'Do you need a lift?'

It was the porter with the wheelchair following me. He had an idea I wouldn't make it back to my room.

Loads of friends and clients came to visit me in hospital, and others phoned Judy and asked if I needed anything. Her answer was food, he is not getting enough to eat at mealtimes. That was true, farriers do tend to have a big appetite, including me.

Andy came to visit me one night with his then-girlfriend. I had just been fed the hospital's small helping for tea, and lunch was about the same sized small portion too. Andy informed me that they were going for a Chinese meal after visiting me. That made my stomach rattle more than ever but gave me an idea.

'Do you think you could get me a Chinese takeaway before you go for your meal?' I asked Andy.

'What time does visiting finish?' Andy asked.

'They don't seem to bother in these rooms off the wards too much as long it is not mega late,' I said.

Three-quarters of an hour later, I was enjoying a Chinese meal thanks to Andy. I didn't know if it was against the rules, but I destroyed the evidence pretty quick, and Andy left with the packaging it came in.

Hospital ended up lasting six weeks full time and then two weeks part time. Why I say part time is that I was allowed to go home on a Friday afternoon and report back Monday morning because of the high dosage of methotrexate that I was on.

It was a time in hospital when I started to think, *Why me?* and feeling a little depressed. A television program pulled me out of it. It was a documentary about a guy in his early thirties who was flying a light aircraft which crashed, leaving him paralysed from the waist down. When he left hospital, his attitude was, *This is me now, I had better make the most of my life*. He didn't look back at what he had had, he looked forward to what he had now. He had a young family and found himself a job so he could support his wife and children. The car was adapted for him to drive, and he got on with enjoying his life.

To this day, I think of that programme when psoriasis flares up. I don't allow myself to get depressed, I think about the guy paralysed getting on with life. I can still walk; he can't. I was able to run and play football with my son Chris; he can never walk, never mind run again. I could do lots of things without thinking about it, but to him it would be a major operation. While watching that programme, I thought to myself, *Why am I getting depressed? At least I will get over psoriasis where I can still walk, he never will.*

Two months after entering hospital, I was allowed to back to work but although I didn't feel sore, I still had a few patches of psoriasis. I could live with that. The methotrexate certainly helped, but the side effects did give my body a bit of a bashing.

For five years I did have small flare-ups now and then, but nothing to stop me working. Again, it had been more of an unsightly irritating nuisance more than anything. The beginning of October 1982, I noticed small eruptions starting to get worse by the day. Within a week, I was covered. Some days I would smother my shirt in Vaseline just to keep my dry, scaly skin moist. I didn't care what people thought about my greasy shirt or jeans, but if that was what I had to do to earn a living, that's what I had to do. My worry was, will it be another hospital job, or will it just peak and go away.

OVERDRAFT

Eighteen months after the bank manager's lecture, I bumped into him one night at a function hosted by one of our wealthy clients. I made a point of having a chat with him and was hoping he remembered me. I was keen to tell him his experience had let him down and we were making money. He did remember me and said if I made an appointment to see him, he could arrange overdraft facilities for us.

My reply was, 'Overdraft facilities? Why do we need an overdraft? We have money in the bank. We are in the black. You bank managers are all the same; once we have proved we don't really need money and we're not skint, we can borrow whatever we want,' I said with a laugh.

'You were a bad risk when you applied,' he replied

'Not as bad as a couple of businesses we both know about,' I answered.

He knew what I meant. Two small hosiery businesses had gone bankrupt, owing thousands. I knew one owner who had told me things were not good and doubted if he was ever going to be in the black, and he banked at the same bank as me. I enjoyed telling him after the lecture he gave us that one way or another we set out to prove him wrong. To be fair to him, he was pleased his judgement of us was wrong and we were making a good living.

I also told him the lecture he gave us probably helped to fire us up even more, as we were determent to prove him wrong. I told him we took on painting farm barns to lorry driving just to keep our heads above water until we built our farriery business.

Around that time we did work for a retired bank manager, who I will call John. While shoeing his horses, I was telling John how we were refused overdraft facilities when we started in business skint. Now we can have one if we want but we had got money in the bank. He smiled then tried to justify why our guy couldn't give us one. Again I said to him that once we had proved we were not skint, we could borrow whatever amount we wanted in reason.

Years later, John wanted a bridging loan to buy a property abroad and the bank were giving him a bit of a headache over his finances. He knew he was coming into money once his late mother's probate was granted but his bank manager didn't want to know. I said to him, 'I know, once you get hold of your mum's money, they will give you your bridging loan.'

He smiled as he remembered my predicament a few years earlier when I moaned to him that once I got money in my bank account, I was entitled to overdraft facilities.

SECOND APPRENTICE

Just short of two years after starting in business, we had enough work to take on a second apprentice, Willy Williams. His real name was Neil but everybody called him Willy. (No relation to John.) Looking back now I can't believe we were in a position to take two apprentices in such a short time after all the obstacles we had to overcome. I had known Willy's family for many years from shoeing their many ponies and horses. Willy, like Paul, came on a six-month trial to see if he fitted in with us and us with him, although like I said with Paul, he just turned up every day. Like Paul, he was a good rider. He, too, often competed with horses and ponies that other horse riders couldn't ride through their frisky nature, with winning results at shows.

I remember one time after shoeing a horse that belonged to a member of a well-known band from Leicester who at the time had lots of hit singles in the 1970s. He bet Willy £5 that he wouldn't be able to ride his horse right round the field. So Willy did without any trouble and true to his word, he was paid the £5. We asked, why did he bet him, what was the catch? It turned out every time the guy got on the horse's back, it tossed him off before getting halfway round the field. The horse seemed to know its owner was a novice, and Willy wasn't.

As for me taking on Willy, it was while shoeing his parent's horses, his father often pestered me that we needed another apprentice like his son. Sure enough his pestering paid off and Willy was made our second apprentice.

With me still living at Whissendine then and 15-odd miles from our forge at Mountsorrel, and Willy nearby, he would make his way to my home and we would travel to the forge or straight to stables together. Paul lived two miles from the forge, and we got into a routine where he worked with Andy and me with Willy. After a while we found that one pair of us would make horseshoes in the morning and the other in the afternoon. OK, one or two occasions we all could be in the forge together, and at really big yards all four of us would. Most of the time though I worked with Willy and Paul with Andy. With two lads coming from horsey backgrounds, it didn't take long before Willy, like Paul, could make a good set of horseshoes.

Before Willy came to work for us, I was not sure we needed anybody else. Most of the time Paul would have gone with Andy and I was quite happy working on my own. It was only when Willy's dad kept pestering me and Andy thought I ought to have some help considering the hours I was working, I gave in. Then I found I appreciated his company and help through the day. Not only that, we were getting more new customers.

Willy approach to the horses was slightly different to Paul's. Although he didn't shout and bawl at a horse that wanted to be difficult while being shod, he would have a little whisper in the horse's ear.

He did this at one yard where a horse tried to be difficult only when the lady owner, I will call Jill, was about. We never wanted her near when we shod her horses as they always seemed to play up when she was nearby. Usually we sent Jill in to make a coffee just to keep her out of the way, and they would behave themselves perfectly. It was only when she was trying to help that they played us up.

On one occasion, Jill was cleaning out her stables and as usual one horse was trying its best to give us grief. Willy didn't realise Jill was near when the horse started to play up. He grabbed the horse's ear and whispered in its ear and it seemed to understand every word what he said, and straight away it behaved itself. (I don't believe the twist he gave at the same time had anything to do with it!) Jill happened to hear him say something, not realising that he got the nag's ear in a tight grip, and was so impressed, and asked what he whispered in the horse's ear to make it behave itself.

To which he replied, 'I told the horse if it didn't behave, I will have to put an ounce of lead in its left ear.'

'Putting an ounce of lead in the horse's left ear makes the horse behave itself then?' she asked.

'Yes, permanently.'

'Oh really, how interesting, and how is this lead inserted in the horse's ear?' she asked with great interest.

'Usually with a shotgun,' replied Willy.

Of course it was just pure luck the horse behaved itself, unless twisting its ear had got more than what he had said to it.

WORKING WITH WILL

Now we were working in pairs, we had a system where Willy and I worked shoeing horses in the morning and made shoes in the afternoon and vice versa with Andy and Paul. Although we had three forges, it became difficult if one of us had to share a forge fire. So it worked better when one pair was out shoeing the horses and the other two shoemaking. Of course there were days when all four of us would meet up at any big stables where there were lots of horses to do.

I can remember one afternoon I took a phone call and it was from a lady client that Andy and Paul were going to shoe for next day. She only wanted to know if they would have time to fit an extra horse in. I told her I am sure they would and I would leave a message for him. I didn't know if he was coming back to the forge before we went home or not but I would ring him later at his lodgings. If we hadn't seen each other before we finished a day's work, we always spoke on the phone in the evening about what work Judy had booked in anyway.

That afternoon it was about five thirty when Willy and I were leaving for home, and we hadn't gone far when we met Andy and Paul coming towards us. I stuck my arm out of the van window to flag Andy down. He braked and pulled up with two wheels on the pavement.

I was further down the road and had got out and started to walk to Andy. Andy had other ideas and put his motor into reverse and stuck his head out of the driver's window and reversed full pelt back to me. Unfortunately, he did not see the lamp post on the van passenger side and he hit it. Yes, you have guessed, the van stopped and his head didn't until it crashed into the window frame. He also put a nice crease from top to bottom in one of the vans back doors. When I got there with Willy, Andy was unconscious, he had knocked himself out when his head hit the door window frame. With Paul living near our forge, he took Andy back to his home, and after a short time, he seemed to recover although with a throbbing headache to get himself back to his digs. Next day, although a bit groggy, he managed a day's work and the extra horse.

ANDY LEAVES

At the beginning of 1979, Andy decided he wanted to go on his own and leave the partnership. He had got married to Jacky two or three months previously and wanted to live and work nearer to where they were living. That being on the other side of Melton Mowbray, further away from our forge at Mountsorrel. Jacky was a local who was from the area, I could understand where he was coming from. I didn't blame him and told him he had got to do what's right for him.

We wished each other the best and agreed I would keep both lads on. At the time, rumours were doing the rounds that we couldn't get on with each other and were always arguing. Well that couldn't have been further from the truth, we didn't fall out, we remained best of friends, even to this present day. OK, I wondered how much work would go with Andy but I was still confident that I would still have enough work for the three of us.

There were odd times when Andy needed extra help and I could manage our workload with just Willy, and Paul would go and help Andy out. Mind you, it was just once in a blue moon when he asked.

After Andy left, Willy and I still did our usual Wednesday round near to where we lived, and most times we never got near the forge at Mountsorrel.

So Paul would spend all Wednesdays making horseshoes for the rest of the week, seeing as he lived nearby. As the months progressed, he had learnt the art of fitting and nailing on. When he reached his last year, the rules of the trade allowed me to leave him to shoe a horse by himself, although he could do so long before as long as I was in attendance. So some days I would arrange one or two horses to be shod at the forge for a change of scenery for him. Sometimes the odd client would ring the forge or call in on the off chance to see if he could help them out. Often clients asked was Paul at the forge on Wednesday, and if they got their nag there, would he shoe it for them. Especially if it was an emergency.

It was when he started shoeing on his own is when I bought another van, I could organise work for him. I am sure he was like me and would sooner have been out fitting the horses with new shoes rather than stuck in the forge making them.

Sometimes I would ask Paul if he could go to so-and-so stables that was in the middle of the countryside. He had probably been there loads of times with me driving but when Paul was a passenger, he never took any notice where the stables were. So when I asked him one day if he could call in at one of these stables in the outback, he would say, 'Where is it? How do I get there?'

Sometimes I would draw a little diagram and hope for the best, although he did always manage to get to where he was going.

Another tactic was to send my son Chris with him as he often came to work with me in his school holidays. Even though he was only eight or nine at the time, he knew where most clients were and which roads led to them. So if Paul couldn't remember the route, I would get Chris to show him the way. It was easier than explaining it to him. Of course, the more he went on his own, he had less problems.

House and forge

Four years after starting the business with no money, Judy and I were now in a position where we could look for our own house to buy. It was 1980 when we started to search for a property near my rented forge to save me 30-mile round trips every day. On our limited budget we found it was not easy to find something as surveys produced some problem or other. That was why they were going cheap. The first house I spotted was an end of terrace three-bedroom house two minutes away from the forge. Seeing a large crack in an outside wall, I got a builder friend Pete to check it over. The verdict was: don't touch it, it needs underpinning, plus next doors too. That sounding expensive so we decided to leave well alone.

The next one was great. A nice little 1930s semi-detached, with a pretty big garden. Much better than the first one. This house looked well maintained, in fact we could have moved in without doing anything to it. It was while we were waiting for the survey, I was excitedly telling one of my clients called Alan where we were hoping to move to. Alan was not impressed when I told him where our new home-to-be was. He said he could understand why the occupants were selling the house and moving.

'I bet they can't get away quick enough,' he stuttered.
'Why? What do you know that I don't?' I replied.

'In that particular area of the village, if it's not tied down it will disappear. God, there are some rough folk who live up there, if that same house was anywhere else but there it would go for a lot more,' he said, shaking his head.

He was right, I had started to investigate what he had told me and everybody I spoke to said they wouldn't want to live there, it's not safe, or words to that effect. Judy agreed we would leave well alone and looked at more houses without success, often beaten to a sale or other parties offering more money – gazumped.

In the next year and a half year spent house-hunting and not finding what we wanted, we had managed to save a little more money, and with help from Judy's mother, we decided we could negotiate a bigger mortgage. We then started to look at houses with outbuildings, with the idea I could have my forge at home and save on the rent I was paying. It bothered me the lady who I was renting from wouldn't give me a rent book or a contract, which meant she could tell me to leave without warning. She knew how desperate we were for something better than the chicken shed. Besides the rent and shoeing her horses for free was more than the place was worth. We felt with no rent money to pay we could put towards a house, and I could then charge her to shoe her horses. Also she never stopped nagging me to build this wall and I felt I couldn't keep up the excuses much longer. I had visions of her saying if I was not building it, I had better leave by the weekend.

Any house we bought now would need planning permission and I found that to be a trial with planning departments. The first house with suitable outbuildings for a forge was perfect, in the middle of the countryside and just about within our budget. The country road leading to it was so isolated that it had grass growing down the middle. With the property up a track, we saw no planning problems. It was typical, no other buyers were interested and our planning permission didn't take long at all to be returned with a decisive: REFUSED.

The reason given for the refusal was that the council's policy stipulated new businesses had to use industrial estates, not in the country. We were fuming, we had no neighbours to upset and horses and industrial estates don't go together. I did go and see the planning officer and asked did he know what a farrier did.

'Yes, a furrier deals with furs,' he stated.

'You are right there, a furrier does deal with furs, but I am not a furrier, I am a farrier, I shoe horses. I don't do anything else, no blacksmithing, I only make horseshoes and fit them to horses' hooves, horses and industrial estates don't go together. It would only take a lorry to clatter past and spook the animal. Someone could get hurt,' I answered in an annoyed voice.

'Can't see much call for horseshoeing in this day and age,' he grunted, not at all interested in what I did for a living.

'Well, why am I trying to put an eight-day week into seven?' I argued.

His answer was I could appeal but doubted I would be successful. Judy and I decided there was no point, they had already made their mind up not to grant planning permission,

Planning permission was refused on another house by a planning department not in the same borough as the last one. The excuse I was refused this time was that an explosion could occur when I welded rotten car chassis up. Again I tried to tell the planning officer I didn't weld rotten car chassis, I didn't even repair my own cars, I hated repairing cars. I only made and fitted horseshoes; if my own vehicles needed attention, the local garage is called. Again we were told we could appeal but there was no point as another buyer had had an offer accepted.

I was coming to the conclusion that we were never going to own our house and forge at this rate. There were always seemed to be problems, it was either the major issues with surveys where the mortgage lender was not happy or losing out to other buyers due to stupid refusals by the planning department.

We finally found a house with an outbuilding at Sileby, two miles from Mountsorrel. This house was about 150 years old with two derelict one-up and one-down cottages, dating back to the sixteenth century, attached. It was the outbuilding which caught our eye. Ted, my brother-in-law who worked in the building construction industry, was sure we could turn it into a forge. We knew we had got competition for it, as a doctor wanted to convert the house and derelict cottages into a doctor's surgery. We found out he hadn't committed to the sale in case planning for a surgery was not successful. Not wanting to lose the chance, we offered the same money as the doctor to start the buying procedure immediately. We took a chance our planning permission would be successful after we had moved in.

Things took a turn for the better when I was shoeing a horse for one of my clients, a retired army colonel who just happened to be the Lord Lieutenant of Leicestershire at the time. I was having a moan to him about all the red tape Judy and I had in the last couple of years attempting to buy our first property. This time though, we were praying we would get planning permission granted after we had gone ahead and bought our Sileby home.

We had already completed the sale and moved in when I spoke to the colonel. He asked me if we had applied for planning. This we had done, I told him, but we couldn't afford to wait for the outcome of whatever the planning officer's decision might be. We thought the doctor would get his planning application results first and we would lose out. What worried me though was what I would do if I was refused yet again; I felt like packing up and moving abroad where businesses are encouraged without stupid obstacles preventing me, I had moaned to the colonel.

He then said, 'Can't have that, Mick, I'll have to see if I can put a spanner in the works.'

I then had an idea the colonel was on my side and he was going to speak up for me. Two or three weeks later, we found our planning application was successful and this time the gamble paid off.

At a later appointment, when shoeing the colonel's horses, he asked, 'Did you get planning for your forge, Mick?'

'Yes, we did,' I answered.

'I thought you might,' the colonel said with a grin on his face.

Five years after starting out in business, we finally swapped our council house for our own home. Now with planning permission one of the first jobs was to convert an outbuilding into a forge. Ted, my brother-in-law, gave me a hand. One of the first jobs was to knock down a dividing wall to make a bigger working area and lay a concrete floor. Once the wall had been demolished, the next job was to dig out the dirt floor ready to lay concrete. It took us all one Sunday and a Monday night after work to dig a metre down through the soil floor to prepare the floor for a concrete base, plus finding problems we had to overcome. I wanted to get a load of ready mix to be delivered on a Saturday morning to make life easier.

Ted insisted and said, 'No, let's mix it ourselves, I am sure we can get it down in one night.'

He was right, we did get the floor concreted, and the next evening we built a coke hopper to store my forge's coke. I don't know how we did it and managing a full day's physical work. Both of us still starting our day jobs at seven in morning no matter what time we finished altering my forge. Sometimes we had less than four hours' sleep.

Ted was right, with laying the concrete and building a coke store after work, it freed up the weekend to empty my old forge. Ted owned a Transit-type pickup truck, and with one of my vans, we managed to empty the old forge in one weekend with the help of Paul and one of his friends. I was half hoping the lady who owned the old workshop was not about because I had kept my mouth shut to her that I had bought my own place. I didn't want her to know until I was ready. This was not made easy when had she had persistently told me to build a stone wall around the old forge for her – at my expense. I felt I had no choice but to stall her with different excuses when she kept asking about the start date for building the wall. Often, I tried answering how builders had let me down or couldn't come for a month. Anything that came into my head to give me more time.

I must have used loads of different excuses for a year or more. I had a feeling if she knew I was planning to leave, she who have wanted me out there and then.

That weekend we not only emptied my old forge but got my new one up and running, ready to start work on the Monday morning. The rent was due on the old workshop a few days later so I called to say I didn't need it anymore. I had an idea that I may be greeted with a not amused lady. I was right, she went mad that I never told her of my plans and I owed a month's notice money. I soon pointed out there was no contract or rent book, and I had been caught out before when I gave notice and was made to leave before the time was up (leaving my last job to start a business) all through not having a contract. She also asked, does this mean she was not getting a wall built and will she have to pay for her horses to be shod.

'Afraid so,' I replied.

Our new home

When I started working for myself in May 1976, I felt owning our own place would never happen. At that time I had trouble raising £50, never mind the thousands I needed to buy 12 Albion Road, Sileby. It became my home and forge for the next 23 years. Judy and I did work on our home over the years. First making the house on the outside look all one house instead of it looking like three. We had disagreements what to do with the inside of the derelict cottages, so they stayed derelict inside for years afterwards and used as storage space. She wanted to turn them into a utility room and shed space but to me it felt as if they were filling up with stuff that we didn't really want. It was too easy just to dump anything that one day may be useful where the local tip may have been a better option. I wanted to knock through and make the two cottages downstairs into one big living room and guest bedrooms upstairs. Then move the kitchen to the front of the house where our old living room and dining rooms were. This meant knocking out another wall to make the two rooms into one so we could have a kitchen diner and the old kitchen to become the utility laundry room. With Judy against my idea, nothing got done.

Thirteen years after buying Sileby, our marriage ran into difficulty. Judy and I were not getting on and called it a day in 1994. She left, and I lived with my two sons after our divorce. Four years after our divorce, I met Phyl (Phyllis) and we got married in 1999. I had mentioned to Phyl what my plans were for renovating the old cottages and moving the kitchen. She thought it was a wonderful idea. We found a wonderful builder called John Robertson who was a first-class tradesman, and his worker Phil, who did a spectacular job. The derelict cottages became a cosy living room and guest apartment beyond our wildest dreams. A year later our kitchen was moved to the front of our home, with John and Phil doing the most spectacular job again.

Holidays

The first four years in business, I never had a holiday. The first year was due to a lack of money, having used our limited funds for starting up the business. During the second year, I was hospitalised for two months, covered from head to toe with psoriasis. I don't know if it was stress from all the many obstacles we had to overcome from starting our own business that brought the outbreak on. Both Andy and I had been working all hours of the day and night just to earn whatever we could to make ends meet. Even then, when work was coming in thick and fast, I still didn't think a holiday was on the cards. I had got it into my head we couldn't afford to lose clients. If we were not on hand, would they use another farrier and stay with him after our break?

It was hard on Andy in the second year when I was having my break from work being laid up in Leicester's General Hospital. Although we had taken Paul on as an apprentice, it was blooming hard work to keep everything together, a holiday was out of the question for Andy too. Paul had only reached the stage of pulling shoes off and clenching up, although he had mastered the making of a good horseshoe, he was still limited to what he could do to help Andy with the actual fitting.

By the summer of 1980, Andy had left the partnership a year before to venture on his own. Paul was starting his fourth year and Willy his third year, and I felt I could manage a week's holiday. So the first family holiday I had in four years was in a tent in a force eight gale, on the Norfolk coast. We were joined by Judy's sister and her husband and her two children and some of their friends on a very sandy campsite. Trying to secure our tents into sandy ground in hurricane conditions was just short of impossible. We used every peg we had trying to secure it to stop them taking off. Positioning our vehicles to act as a windbreak worked a little but often at night we thought, *Was the tent going to be with us in the morning?* It never did take off in the strong winds, but it was a constant battle to stop them becoming airborne. We also used breeze blocks or big logs to anchor the tents to the ground and hoped that they were still there when we left them in the daytime.

It was a holiday that was supposed to get me away from work. I had been (and still am) told not to look at a horse's hooves to see how well or not they are shod when I am not working. I can't seem to help myself. But on this particular day, a Saturday, all of us had visited a museum where different people were working on machinery from years gone by. There was a lady demonstrating weaving on an old spinning jenny. A potter at work, also a guy doing amazing things turning wood on his lathes, which consisted no more than string and a block of wood to act as a foot pedal. Along with all the other attractions, I heard the sound of a hammer and anvil noise. I found two guys working in a forge making gate hooks and after watching them, it soon became apparent they were not professionals. More like a bank clerk or manager, I thought, but I was nearly right as they both were accountants. The forge fuel was bits of big chunks of coal, making their fire dirty and smoky. It took an age to get any sort of heat and the gate hooks were more like a bit of a bent bar of steel. They then tried to instruct me how to make gate hooks, well that is when I told them they wanted what we call farrier's breeze. This is small coke and is cleaner and easier to work and did they want me to give them a crash course in forging skills. I told them I had a forge of my own but I made horseshoes.

One guy looked me up and down and said, 'Wait here, I think we need your help,' and walked off.

I thought he was had gone to find a boiler suit or some sort of protective clothing to protect my holiday attire. All the other guy said was I would be appreciated. My first thought, I was going to be giving these two guys a crash course in how to make gate hooks until I heard the sound of a horse clip-clopping with very loose horseshoes attached to its feet. It was an old carthorse with a cart still attached to it that was used to give rides to the museums customers.

It was accompanied by its owner plus the owner of the museum. They wanted me to refit its shoes as its hooves were getting a little overgrown.

I said, 'Look, I am on holiday and I have not got any kit.'

To which they replied, 'We have, please help us out. We're getting desperate.'

I looked at Judy, and she stared back at me, and we both thought, what the hell, I will shoe the old horse for them. I asked if I could come back later as I wanted to change my clothes. I knew I had got a pair of jeans which were soon to be working clothes back at the tent, plus a shirt which was far from new.

I was asked if I could come back the next day (Sunday), around two o'clock in the afternoon. So all of us went back on the Sunday as Judy's sister's friends had never seen a horse shod before. When we arrived at the museum, we could see why the museum boss said two o'clock that afternoon. It had given him time to erect signs advertising a farrier demonstration. I was going to be one of the star attractions.

The two guys had got the forge lit with a bag of coke instead of coal. (Not farrier's breeze but at least it was better than coal.) When I saw the kit I had got to work with, I thought, *Oh my god.*

The hoof paring knife was blunt. The clippers for trimming the horse's feet were some ancient contraption for trimming cows' feet. As for the rasp for levelling the foot and finishing off, well I think I had thrown better ones away.

I knew at least I didn't have to make new shoes as I was only taking the old ones off and refitting, but I was going to be the star attraction. Was it going to end up as a great big bodge?

The horse and its owner arrived minus the cart and we were surrounded by a crowd of fifty-odd people. The tools I had been supplied with were in a heap on the ground. I was used to having my kit all together in a specially made toolbox.

Getting the horse's four shoes off was easy, it was paring the foot that was the hardest. The hoof clippers, although they clipped the hoof OK, I found them to be heavy and cumbersome. Rasping the foot level, I found if I used the side edge of the worn-out rasp I got some sort of result, as the flat edge's teeth were well worn. The two guys who worked the forge had got the shoes hot while I dressed the horse's hooves, and although I needed to adjust them, the fitting was easy. Now to nail them on.

'Where are the nails?' I asked one of the guys working the forge. I need number tens.'

'What do you mean tens?' he asked.

'Horse nails come in different sizes, the smaller the shoe, you use smaller nails, the bigger ones, we use larger nails,' I replied, thinking this job is turning into a comedy sketch, and soon the crowd might be booing.

'Ooh, I don't know, I will go and find out,' and he clears off to find if they have any horse nails. I got visions of him finding a bag of nails used for nailing wood together. Nails for horseshoeing are shaped different and specially made.

He appeared with a wooden box full of assorted sizes. To my relief they were for horseshoeing. I found the box contained a mixture of most sizes and enough number tens and eights for me to start nailing the first shoe on. I got the idea I may have to use a mixture of these nail sizes. I got the two guys searching for what I needed while I nailed the first shoe on. With the shoes having been a refit, I got by using a smaller nail where the shoe was slightly worn at the toe. Eventually I got the old horse shod to a round of applause off the crowd. I don't know if they thought the same as me and had been entertained by a load of idiots or what.

The museum owner gave a little speech as the demonstration was something different. He was right on that score and everybody clapped again. Then he turned to me and wanted to pay me, and so did the guy who owned the horse. Back then, charges were probably something like ten pounds for a new set and eight for a refit. (Nowadays, it's 70 pounds upwards, shire horses were more around 12 to 15 pounds, now into the hundreds.) Well the museum bloke had 25 pounds in his hand and so did the horse owner, and both men started arguing about who wanted to pay me. After a minute or so, the museum owner took the 25 pounds from the horse owner and gave me his 25 pounds too and said, 'Here, take the lot.'

I thought Christmas had come early, 50 quid for an hour's work, equivalent to 250 pounds today. Some folk were barely earning that in a week then.

I wondered did they want me to shoe more horses!

RETURN FROM HOLIDAY

While I was on my Norfolk holiday, I did ring the lads occasionally from a phone box to check that they were coping OK. (No mobiles then.) Willy had answered and told me a Mrs Baxter had rung that morning and wanted some shoes taken off one of her ponies quick as it had to be measured. He said he would fit it in on his way home. Other than that everything was OK and no problems had arisen. He told me to enjoy my holiday as there was nothing to worry about. So when I returned and true to what Willy had said, the two of them had coped without me.

The first Monday morning after my holiday, I had a phone call off Mrs Baxter, wanting the shoes put back on the pony Willy had taken off while I was away and another one to shoe. She also had to have a moan about Willy turning up at half past six in the evening to take the shoes off the week before.

'I thought you only rang him up in that morning, he did his best to squeeze you in at such short notice, and he thought he was doing you a favour,' I protested.

'Well, I don't want you turning up late in the afternoon. I prefer a morning appointment,' and put the phone down before I had chance to say which day I could book her in.

A few minutes later, Mrs Baxter was back on the phone again to find out which day I was going to make an appointment for her.

'You want a morning, I have a space in a week tomorrow, but if you didn't mind an afternoon, I could fit you in Wednesday this week.'

I knew damn well she would go for the afternoon appointment even though we could have done a swap with someone and gone to her in the morning.

On the Wednesday afternoon, I and the two lads visited Mrs Baxter, and to fit the shoes back on the pony Willy had taken off was easy, but the other one which she was selling was another story. She had buyer for it, but at its new home the farrier couldn't shoe it because it was too wild. We found out she sold it to be good to shoe, box and clip. I don't know what it was like to clip but judging by its coat, not very good. As for shoeing, it had never seen a set of shoes in its life. The thing was mad.

She told the new owners she was sure we could shoe it, and if we could the sale would stand. Well four hours later, we did get shoes on with the help of a vet who had turned up to look at one of her other horse's welfare. He tried sedation, but with the pony already in a strop, the injection didn't work. So Michael the vet, who was a big stout fellow, held it similar to how a wrestler holds their opponents in a headlock and after a big struggle we got four shoes on, and Mrs Baxter had a sale.

It was six o'clock when we finished. I had only allowed an hour to shoe both but never expected a battle like we had. Mrs Baxter was over the moon with us as the sale of the pony stood, now we had got shoes on it. I then thought she must have had a bad day over Willy arriving in the evening as she wasn't complaining about us still on her yard. Well I was wrong; she found something else to complain about, the bill. She wanted me to deduct what Willy charged her when he took the pony's shoes off while I was on holiday. Her argument was we didn't have shoes to take off, only to refit. I tried to reason with her that was a separate job. He still had to travel there. Besides this wild pony we have shod for her took the three of us three hours plus, and I had charged the normal rate. Other yards, we could have shod four or five horses in the same time it took to do her one pony. This lady never gave it a thought how difficult her pony was or if one of us got hurt. She did pay me, although I could see she was not happy about it.

A few days later I was at another yard when the client, I will call Beth, told me Mrs Baxter had been talking to her about me. I thought she was going to say how Mrs Baxter was pleased with us for shoeing her wild pony, but she didn't. Mrs Baxter wasn't amused with my charges.

'What? Did she tell you it took me and my two lads three hours plus to shoe a pony another farrier couldn't get near? I supposed she told you I was robbing her as I wouldn't deduct what Willy charged for going out of his way and taking off the pony's shoes a week or so before,' I moaned.

'Don't worry, Mick, I know you too well. I knew there was something she wasn't telling me,' replied Beth.

I decided there and then that was the last pony I would shoe for Mrs Baxter. We had had other problems with her before. One was she never seemed to be ready for us when we arrived. Often her horses were still out in the field and we would be hanging around waiting for one of her staff trying to round them up. It didn't matter if she made us late for our next appointment, but if we were late arriving for her, she played merry hell.

MONICA

Another of my clients was a wonderful lady I will call Monica. I don't know what sort of age she was but if I had to guess, probably middle sixties. Saying that, she looked 60 all the 15 years she was my client. Monica was a tall, very thin lady who hadn't got an ounce of fat on her body. She was a spinster all her life, who spoke in a very refined, soft voice and had all the time in the world for any child who had an interest in her ponies. The kids used to ride her ponies at shows and gymkhanas and although she was very strict, no one said a bad word about her. In fact, she probably had more to do with the many children on weekends than their parents did.

As for me shoeing her ponies, her stables had a big concrete base in front of them, which made it ideal for me shoeing, unlike other stables. Some only had a two-or three-foot-wide hardstanding strip outside, so when the horse or pony was tied up, the back hooves could be standing in mud.

The other thing was, Monica could be a problem. She would want to help me with the shoeing and would like to hold her ponies headcollar. Instead of holding the animals loose, she held them as if she was a professional wrestler. I kept saying to her, 'Tie them up, they will be fine, I am sure there is no need to put a half nelson hold on them.'

No, she would insist, which in turn made the ponies struggle. She thought it was her nags that were behaving badly but if for some reason she wasn't there, the kids would tie them up and I would shoe them without any trouble. Monica couldn't see she was the problem.

Although she spoke in a soft, refined tone, she didn't mind a friendly joke or me pulling her leg with what I call polite cheek. Her voice, though, would get to almost a whisper if she didn't approve of how some folk behaved or unsavoury things happing in the news. One day she caught me off guard when she was telling me what happened to her one weekend. She had to tell me she had been invited round to one of her horsey friends having a do one Saturday night. I knew the people in question and what their lifestyle was like.

So Monica had to tell me who was there from the horsey world. It didn't surprise me that some well-known important folk not connected to equine were there too. There were butlers and maids in attendance. A five-course meal and countless bottles of wine were drunk during and after dinner. The guests were treated perfectly. Then she said in a very soft voice almost to a whisper, 'Mick, do you know, Mick. After the meal, all the men put their car keys in a bowl and the lights were dimmed, and the ladies had to put their hands in to pick a set out.'

'What was the idea of that, Monica?' Knowing full well what was happening. It didn't surprise me that the folk in question held these sort of parties as I had heard other stories. I thought Monica was going to tell me that she was disgusted what the entertainment was. She said in a whisper, 'Well, Mick, they were wife swapping. It was a swingers party.'

'Whose husband did you get then, Monica?' I asked.

It's the next bit I got stuck for words when she replied, 'Well, Mick, I had to leave, didn't I?'

'Oh, why was that, Monica?' and another *Well, Mick*.

'Well, Mick, (voice gets lower), how could I stay? Because I didn't have a husband to swap,' she replied with a serious look on her face.

That was the bit that took me by surprise. If she had had a husband, would she have stayed?

STOCKHOLM TAR

One freezing cold winter's day, I arrived to shoe a horse that belonged to a young lady I will call Masie. She lived with her parents in a three-bed semi-detached on the edge of a village just outside Leicester. Her horse lived in a field nearby and usually I shod it in the field gateway during the summer months. With the amount of rain we had that winter it was a no-go area, especially for horseshoeing due to the amount of mud. So Masie arranged for me to shoe her horse at her parents' house backyard where there was hardstanding.

That particular day when I arrived, her dad, Ray, was in a bit of a paddy. Masie told me she had trouble with an infection in her horse's frogs. (A horse's frog is the bit of rubbery like tissue in the middle of a horse's hoof.) She was sure the wet soggy field her horse was turned out in didn't help and wanted to plaster the frog in Stockholm tar when I had finished shoeing her horse. A year or so before, I had once said that Stockholm tar may work on another problem her horse had, and she thought it may act as a barrier against the wet, muddy field her horse lived in. It was well known to help keep infection away. The downside is it can be messy and difficult to clean if you accidentally spill it on your hands or surfaces.

The first thing Ray said to me was I was in trouble for recommending Stockholm tar.

'Why, what have I done?' I asked.

Then a little grin came on his face, he said, 'Come in the house and have a look at this.'

When I entered, the aromas of petrol filled my nostrils. Then I saw a black sticky substance covering the fireplace, carpet, three-piece suite, sideboard, walls and the dog. Masie then told me what had happened. The tin lid of the Stockholm tar was stuck on solid from not being used for a year or so and her dad had the bright idea of putting it next to the coal fire. He thought it may turn the hardened-off tar causing the lid to be stuck fast to turn into liquid. It worked too well when he left it next to the fire longer than he should have. It exploded. Luckily the family, apart from the dog, were in the kitchen when they heard the explosion. They too may have got covered in the sticky substance if they were in the room. It was amazing how a tin of hot Stockholm tar could decorate a whole living room in seconds.

When Ray tried to clean up, he found the more he rubbed, the tar seemed to expand. He tried one cleaning product then another but nothing worked until one of his mates suggested petrol. Although it was slow progress, it seemed to be working, but it meant sitting in coats in the evening as they didn't dare light the fire. In the end, he ended up giving his living room a full makeover.

PAUL LEAVING

It was May 1982 when Paul came to me and said he wanted to leave as he been offered a position still as a farrier at a large racing stables. He had become fully qualified nine months before and felt he couldn't turn the job down and gave me a month's notice. It didn't surprise me because I had wanted to do the same thing when I was his age. The only thing that was different was that he did something about it and I didn't. I had only talked about leaving my job at Derek's then.

Again there was no fallout, I just wondered if I wanted to take on another apprentice to replace him or to make my business smaller. It was not that I was struggling for work but more that I had got too much. Sometimes I felt I was neglecting my family life always working. I wanted to be like other dads and go with my son to watch him play football on Saturday mornings and watch Leicester City play at their home games instead of somebody else's dad taking Chris with their sons. Did I want a big business? After all, the bigger it is, the bigger the overheads, and I would still be no better off salary wise.

I spoke to Judy and Willy as he would be away at college to take his final exams to become a fully-fledged farrier soon. I knew I was due for an increase in prices due to yearly inflation and thought I would increase my price a couple of quid more than usual, and maybe one or two clients will drop out. I didn't want to decide who I should drop; I wanted the client to decide if they wanted my services. My way of thinking was to work less hours but still have the same income. In practice, that was the idea. Well it didn't work out like that. All my clients still wanted me to shoe their horses and just moaned about my charges.

I did eventually decide that every other Saturday I would book nothing in and watch Chris play football.

Less than a year later, Willy was having a few problems in his life and having just passed his farrier exams, wanted to try his hand working for himself. At the time I was having a flare-up with psoriasis. I thought then I was glad I had not made my business any bigger and years later I found out I was just as well off as other farriers who had employed more help. I didn't have the worry like others did looking for work when foot and mouth hit the job. There were places we were not allowed to go. I only had myself to worry about and didn't have to find wages for my staff.

I also decided the new van I just bought I was going to keep until it gave trouble, and when I did have to replace it, I would get one that was a couple or so years old. After all, the ones I got rid of were still reliable, and it would save me money on the price of a new one every three years. Even the old Anglia had not given too much bother. I would run them until they were old and on their last legs. Also I got fed up with some folk saying I must be raking it in to afford a new one. One farrier once said it was a mistake to arrive at my clients in a banger, as he changed his regularly on lease hire. I asked him why as my old vans I had had before hardly ever let me down. His reply was it would impress clients, they don't like to see you turn up in anything tatty.

'Turn up in a banger? I am sure all my clients wouldn't care if I turned up with my kit in a wheelbarrow as long as they were happy with my work. It's a poor tale if you have to have a new motor to impress people rather than the job you have done on their horse's hooves. After all I got plenty of work when all I could afford was a £35 green Anglia van with wet paintwork,' was my reply.

Not only that, I didn't have to worry about the monthly instalments on the lease of the van, like some did when the foot and mouth epidemic limited where we could work. So when Willy left, I never took any more new clients on and cut down on one or two overheads. Over the years, some clients either moved away or gave up horse riding. Some I got the excuse to give the heave-ho to for being bad at paying. Eventually I got my work to a happy medium. I always had a waiting list of new clients so if one did drop out, I could replace with a new one. I am sure I was just as well off money-wise making my business small with less headaches than if I employed more staff.

COMPANY DIRECTOR'S WIFE

A client, who I will call Vera, had never done a hard day's work in her life. Her husband, though, was a guy who had worked hard to be promoted to a very senior role in the very large company he worked for. Also he praised others who wanted to improve their lifestyle through determination. He knew, when I started out in business, I had nothing, and he appreciated how hard I had worked to get to be able to afford my own house and forge. Unfortunately his wife had the opposite view. I got the impression she didn't like the idea that I could be getting on a little too well for her liking. I think she thought I was getting to be in the same mould as her. She wanted to be able to look down at me like she did with others.

Her husband had the financial clout to give his wife a life where she could have whatever she wanted. She employed a girl to look after her horses, someone to clean her house plus other handymen often seen doing jobs other people would do themselves. They both had a top-of-the-range BMW car plus a vintage Rolls Royce parked in the garage. A very nice property with an acre of land attached. I was not against anybody who had got on in life, but I was not amused when Vera told me I was earning too much money one morning.

That came about when I arrived one morning to shoe one of her horses in my three-day-old Transit van. (The last new one I bought.) The first thing she said was I must be earning too much money to afford a new motor. I pretended I never heard her say it and proceeded to shoe her horse. The old horse had nice round open feet, which was easy to shoe and was one that never seemed to take as long as others. Although I didn't mind Vera's horses, I was not too struck on her as she had said hurtful things to me before, and I tried not to let it bother me.

That day, I didn't realise she was going to be timing me either shoeing her horse which took me 40 minutes. I know others took longer but as I have said, this one seemed easier, and I didn't know it had taken 40 minutes until Vera told me. I think the price at the time was about £17 to fit a full set, and she worked out I must be raking it in at the same rate her solicitor friend charged. I asked if she had timed me making her horse's shoes in my forge at eight o'clock the night before or my travelling time, but she didn't think that time counted.

Other times I had bit my tongue and said nothing, but this time Vera had annoyed me. First over my new van and then telling me I was earning too much money. So I snapped back and said I had worked blooming hard to get my new van. It was part of my toolkit. I didn't own a top-of-the-range BMW or vintage Rolls Royce like she and her husband did. What would she have said if I criticised her for their wealth? How would she have liked it? If I had to phone to say I would have to cancel her appointment due to the old van that had broken down, she would have been the first to say I needed a new one. I didn't begrudge her husband to be able to afford their lifestyle. I admired him. She then told me that her husband had had to pass examinations to get where he is today. I told her I had to pass a stiff examination to be allowed to practise farriery. Whatever she said, I could say 'so have I' and what stopped her husband training to be a farrier if she thought that it earned a better living.

Another tactic was she tried was to get me to shoe her horses first thing on a Monday morning a few years before, around 1977. The price then was maybe around £8. I would shoe one horse for her, and she would want to show off with a 50-pound note to pay me. Her idea was to boast that she dealt with 50-pound notes and hoping I wouldn't be able to give her change. I heard from other tradesmen that she had done the same to them and offered to pay the next time they delivered. Then insist she had paid the time before. Well, when she did it to me, she was out of luck. After I shod her horse, my next port of call was the bank with my takings from the week before. I enjoyed watching the look on her face and said the 50-pound note was no problem and gave her £42 change out of the last week's takings. Another tactic was to apologise she had got no cash and only had one cheque left in her cheque book and she needed it to pay her butcher.

I would say, 'I am here first, pay me and owe the butcher instead.'

By 1988, Vera was still somehow managing to be on my books and still causing me grief. I was still looking at ways to make my business smaller. What I mean by smaller, the area I travelled, and Vera was nearer 20 miles from my forge. I had more than enough work in a 10-mile radius of Sileby. Then after one appointment, Vera gave me the green light to drop her.

It was one busy day when I was hoping all my calls were going to be ready for me. I had bookings all through the day, with the last one at six thirty in the evening. I had a habit of starting my day at the farthest appointment and working my way home. Seeing Vera was the farthest, I had her booked for seven thirty in the morning. On arriving, I found no horse was in its stable and no Vera too. I knew the lady groom she employed was part time and turned up once she had taken her children to school around nine o'clock. Vera's car was not in the drive and I had a good idea she had nipped off somewhere before I arrived and would be back in a minute. The minute turned into half an hour and through experience if I was late at the first call, it didn't matter how I tried, I could never make time up. Time seemed to get faster and I would get later and later as the day went on. I thought if I hung about waiting for her, I had got visions of starting the last call of the day at nine o'clock in the evening. So I cleared off before she showed up.

At seven o'clock while shoeing my last horse, the new car phone I had just got installed in my van rang. It was Vera. Not apologising that her or her horse were not ready for me but was fuming her horse was not shod. I told her I was on time at seven thirty but her horse was not in the stable and she was out. I felt she was trying to belittle me and said I must be stupid and blind not to see her horse in its stable. Well, if she had left the horse in the stable, it must have escaped as the stable door was wide open and so was the front gate, and I had hung about for half an hour. Then she forgot what she had said and that her horse was grazing in the orchard and had expected me to go and catch it. I didn't know they had an orchard and it turned out they hadn't, it was somebody else's in the village. If she thought I was going looking for her nag and traipsing to the end of the village, she better think again. I don't think Vera couldn't help herself and still thought I was at her beck and call. Well I wasn't, and that was when I told her she had better look for another farrier. Then I heard a woman crying her eyes out that I was not going to shoe her horse. I nearly felt sorry for her and should I go back. No, I came to my senses as she would never have given it a second thought earlier that day that she could be causing me to be late for my other appointments.

UNBROKEN PONY

It was while I was away on my first holiday in Norfolk when Paul went off on his rounds by himself. He got two horses at the first call and two at the second, then odd appointments for the rest of the day. At the first stables, he found one of the horses was not well, and the owner decided not to have it shod until it had recovered from whatever it was suffering from. So he was going to be an hour early at his next call, at Mrs Taylor's.

Paul had been to Mrs Taylor's loads of times to shoe her horse but on this occasion, she had booked for somebody else's pony to be shod with her own horse at the same time. On arriving an hour early, he was not surprised to see Mrs Taylor's horse out in the field. She was a lady who was always ready but he could understand why she wasn't this time. He got the idea she was not at home as her car was not in the drive but seeing a pony in the stable, he took it that was the one to be shod.

He found a head collar, and the pony never minded him putting it on. He brought it out of the stable and tied it up to a tie ring. The pony hadn't got any shoes to take off, and Paul soon had its new set fitted without any bother. He just got it put back in the stable and was grabbing a bite of one of his sandwiches when Mrs Taylor appeared and asked was he early or was she late.

He told her, no, she's not late as he only had one horse to shoe instead of two at his last call. She saw hoof clippings, and when she realised he shod the pony, she looked amazed. The way she looked at him, he thought he shod the wrong one until she said it was her friend's pony. How did he manage to shoe it on his own?

'OK, good as gold,' he told her.

Then he got the story how it was unbroken, and Mrs Taylor was dreading it may be difficult to shoe.

Three months later, the forge phone rang one afternoon at about four thirty. The person on the other end asked if we were the farriers who shod her pony at Mrs Taylor's. Paul had never told me he shod an unbroken pony by himself. All I knew was Mrs Taylor had a pony to shoe at the same appointment. I suppose it never entered his head to mention it as the nag was as good as gold. If it was a right pain, he may have said something, but as most stand still and behave, it would never enter his head to say anything.

The caller asked how Paul managed to get shoes on her pony as her farrier can't get anywhere near it without kicking and striking out at him. The shoes Paul put on were still on, and its hooves were now overgrown. That is when I found out what happened when Paul told me he just tied it up and shod it.

I got Paul to speak to the owner seeing as he had shod it, and he couldn't believe it had a nasty streak in it. I heard him ask where she lived and found it to be miles away. Way out of our area. She pleaded if Paul could come and try to shoe the pony again, and she would pay a very generous travelling fee plus the price of a set of shoes even if he failed.

A time and day was sorted and off Paul went to tend to the pony. On his return, he didn't know what the fuss was about as it stood perfectly. He wished every horse and pony were that easy! Even the owners couldn't believe their eyes as Paul wanted to shoe it by himself with no one clinging on to its head collar. They were expecting a bit of a struggle.

Two o'clock appointment

Working with animals, we can never be sure how long each job is going to take. So if a farrier or for that matter a vet books a call for, say, two o'clock, they can only give an approximate time, and I will say why. Although I could more often be on time or thereabouts. At some calls, it could be the horse was not the easiest to shoe behaviour-wise. Or the farrier is having to deal with a complicated problem. It could be anything from having to fit a surgical shoe for a lame horse or something which may be not so straightforward. What did hold me up the most, though, was folk not being ready. For example, a lady I will call Jenny always wanted me every six weeks at two o'clock on a Thursday afternoon to shoe her horse. That was no problem as Jenny would book me after each visit for the next shoeing for six weeks later.

Her horse was easy to shoe, and it behaved itself perfectly for me. The trouble was when it was turned out in a great big field. It never liked Jenny to catch it. Well, most other owners would have thought of this before I arrived and had their horses caught ready for me. Not Jenny, if the appointment was two o'clock, that is when she arrived at her stables. (She lived at the other end of the village from her stables.) Often, I was there waiting, and when she saw me, she would go to her tack room and faff about getting her wellingtons on and change her coat. Then look for the right head collar for her horse. I used to think any head collar would do, but no she got to find the right one. By now 10 minutes would have passed and she had still got to catch the horse. The field the horse was in was on a hill, and the horse was always down at the bottom. Jenny would walk down to the horse, and when she got near the thing, it would take off at the same pace as if it were the Grand National winner back to the top of the paddock. Jenny would stagger back up the slope again and when she got near to it, off the nag would trot back down the slope. By now another 20 minutes would have passed when Jenny would come running back to grab a bucket of pony nuts. Finally after another 10 minutes, she managed to catch it. I am now thinking to myself, *I am going to be mighty late for my next call and a late finish tonight,* all because one client couldn't have their horse ready for me.

Luckily Jenny's horse was good to shoe and I could crack on with it. Then after several episodes of her being not ready, I thought I will still do a two o'clock appointment but tell her the next one is at one o'clock. So next time Jenny got to her stables dead on one, and I am not there. I suppose it took her half an hour before she got her horse caught again. Dead on two o'clock, I arrived, and the first thing she said was, 'You are late.'

I smiled and said, 'I know, the last person couldn't catch their horse. Do you know somewhere else that happens?'

After that, no more was said and Jenny took the hint, and she was ready for me on future appointments.

ONE WET
SATURDAY MORNING

As I have said, Paul often used to turn up to help us on Saturdays or in his school holidays before he started to work for us. Well, the first time he turned up, he was dressed smarter than some kids of today when out socialising in the evenings. I don't know if he was trying to impress us like one does at interviews, but this particular Saturday morning he certainly impressed a pony I had got to shoe.

It was the first time he had come with me on my rounds. That Saturday morning was a damp winter's day with a light drizzle trying its best to get heavier. It was the second call of the morning at a new client, a lady called Joy. She lived with her mother and sister at the time. The three women couldn't have done any more to help me, considering the weather. The only thing that bothered me was, is this drizzle of rain going to get any heavier. There is nothing worse than thinking it's not too bad, then when halfway through, the drizzle changes to a heavy downpour. It is not just with getting soaked but with wet tools and slimy hands, I felt the job lasted forever. The rasp that is used to file the horse's foot level gets bunged up and loses its edge.

Joy had a horse called Gerry and a four-year-old pony named Hipperty to shoe. It was going to be Hipperty's first set of shoes, and Joy was a little worried about how he would behave. Her house had a large stable at the bottom of her large garden and another gate that led into a very muddy paddock next to it. In fact, with all the rain that we just had at the time it was a quagmire.

Joy had not let Gerry and Hipperty out into the paddock that morning as she didn't want them plastered in mud when I arrived. I thought that was very kind of her as other owners would have let them out and would often expect the farrier to clean the horse's legs and hooves when he arrived. The only trouble at Joy's was I couldn't get my van near to the stable. Outside her kitchen back door, though, there was a nice clean concrete area that was ideal for shoeing horses on.

Joy brought Gerry out first. Gerry was a Welsh cob who was about 11 or 12 years old. Although she had put a head collar on him, he would have stood with no one holding on to him. He was a pleasure to shoe. I had him done in no time.

The trouble was when Joy took Gerry back to the stable. (It was big enough for both.) When she opened the door to put Gerry in, Hipperty barged past them and headed for the open gate into the muddy paddock. It looked as if Hipperty had other ideas about being shod. Joy went to catch him, but he was having none of it. In places, she found it difficult to walk, never mind run after her pony, considering how deep this quagmire was. Then things got worse; Joy stepped out of one of her wellington boots. She managed to pull it out of the mud but when trying to put it on, she fell over. In the meantime, Hipperty had decided he wanted a mud bath and got down for a roll in the slime.

Joy by now had changed Hipperty's name to Swine plus many others. After five or ten minutes, he did let her catch him.

He was now covered head to toe in mud, and Joy didn't look much better. Her sister had got the hosepipe out ready to shower Hipperty off and I thought it may be a good idea to do Joy at the same time. It turned out he didn't want to be hosed down either but didn't mind being dried off with towels, so I didn't get too wet.

I picked up my box of tools and tried to get near Hipperty. He was having none of it. The more we tried, the more agitated he got. He stood on his front feet and tried bucking and rearing whenever I got close to him, although he would let Paul near him. He even picked Hipperty's front foot up. Did he know that Paul couldn't shoe him at the time, or was he more interested in the aftershave lotion he wore? He seemed to sniff him out when Paul was near to him.

I had an idea we were not going to get him shod that day, and with the rain getting heavier, I would come back and try another day. Joy's mum thought it was the fact I smelled of wet horse and burning hoof that put him off. So first thing on the Monday morning, dressed in clean clothes and with aftershave lotion splashed on, I cold shod Hipperty without the apron that protected my legs on. (Cold shoeing is where the shoes are not put in a forge and burnt on the foot.) I didn't want to take the chance the apron could have horsey odours on it. Joy's mum said Hipperty liked me to be dressed in clean clothes. So for the next 18 years, that is how I shod Hipperty. I once tried to fit him in at the end of the day, but he was having none of it. I had to wear clean clothes.

Often, I have tried to get into animals thoughts, no matter if it's a dog, cat or horse. I often wondered if Hipperty and Gerry's horsey talk went something like this.

Talking about the farrier:
Hipperty and Gerry

'Morning, Gerry. Oh what a wet day, never mind the nice lady has been and fed us. I like her, she's really kind. Mind you, Gerry, I've heard talk this farrier guy is coming on Saturday morning to fit horseshoes on our feet. God, have you ever had a whiff of him. His damp pullover stinks awful with his cheap burning smelly hoof deodorant, I'm not keen on that. How the hell do you put up with it, Gerry?'

'Oh, Hipperty, once you get to my age, you can't be arsed, let him get on with it. Anyway the quicker he finishes, the more time to ourselves.'

'No, Gerry, you have to have some fun, you learn new words that are not yet part of the English language, but it's that stink what really gets me. Not only that, he tries to set fire to your feet. Don't like that.'

'Hipperty, got news for you; it's Saturday today.'

'Saturday today? Oh no, that means...'

'Yes, that means shoes on feet time.'

'You've made me go all funny, Gerry, I want to go for a roll in the slimy mud in the paddock to chill out.'

'They'll swear at you.'

'Don't care. I love slimy mud in my coat.'

'Hipperty, they'll go spare with you, you will get plastered. Oh, the farrier guy has turned up.'

'I'm not going, they'll have to catch me.'

'OK, Hipperty, I'll go first, you do your own thing.'

'Yep, I'm off for my slimy mud bath, get him to take his time.'

'It's not that bad having your feet manicured and new shoes fitted, Hipperty. In fact, this guy is quite patient and kind. Your turn in an hour. I'll give you a shout when he's finished.'

'Gerry, don't stand still, give him what for, make him earn his money, you are letting him be too quick. Oh Lord, you are nearly finished.'

'Bugger it. Gerry's finished that was quick, they're shouting for me, going for a plodder into the middle of that slimy bog. Changed my mind. I'll stand in the middle of it. I feel a bit sorry for the kind lady, though, but sod it, I'm not shifting, she'll have to come to get me. Oh dearie me, she's stepped out of her wellie. Ooh, she's balancing on one leg trying to get it back on, oops she's fallen over. Don't understand what she's calling me. Yes, I do.'

'What's that, going to wash me down with the hosepipe? Oh no, please don't tie me up, you can't do that, it's freezing. Ooh, no, stop it, I don't like it! Ooh, I like being all muddy. Oh no, be careful where you aim that water jet. Ooh, it's a waste of time. I don't want that farrier guy anywhere near me, he stinks of wet horse, smells as if he's on fire too. Oh, here he comes, must do my dance routine; I'll show him how clever I am to stand on my front feet and kick out with my back ones all at the same time. Did I hear him get my name wrong? It's not YOU SWINE. It's Hipperty. Hang on, who's that young lad who's come with him? He's nice, dressed smarter too. God, that aftershave lotion and deodorant stuff has made me go all weak at the knees. Argh, he's picking my foot up, must have a good sniff of him. Ooh, he smells gorgeous. I'll let him shoe me, but I know he can't.'

'Hey up, what's going on now, can't hear what they're saying. I don't believe it, they're packing the tools away. Eeee showed him, that farrier chap, he's given up on me. Scared him, won't see him again, must tell Gerry.'

'I bet he'll be back, Hipperty, don't count your chickens yet, I heard something about Monday.'

'Monday, what did you hear about Monday?'

'He's coming back Monday when he's got more time.'

Weekend passes.

'Do you think he'll come back, Gerry?'

'You've asked that all weekend, Hipperty, and guess what, he's back.'

'Holy mackerel, Gerry, look at him, he's got clean clothes on. Oh God, what the hell in the name of the Lord has he covered himself with? Deodorant and aftershave lotion, well that's an improvement. Have I gone silly; I quite like him this morning? He has not got that apron thing round his legs; I hope he's not going to wear it. Yep, he can put shoes on me as long as that fire thing is not used. Still going to be a prat though. I'm still going to stand in the slimy mud instead of the clean concrete. That'll show him I haven't given up completely, and that is how he will have to put shoes on my feet for the next 18 years. They can't make an ass out of me!'

A BONE CHINA TEA SET

Most farriers never refuse a brew, in case we never get offered any more refreshment for the rest of the day. At most working stables they had mugs. OK, we often had to drink out of vessels that were a bit chipped or cracked with no handles, but we didn't mind that. Mind you, some of the crockery our cuppa came in looked as if they hadn't had a proper wash, judging by the stains embedded in them.

On one of our calls, the stables were behind the owner's house. They had a big garden with an orchard where the horses grazed. The family that lived there were a couple and their teenage daughter. Again their hospitality was most welcoming as a brew would be made the moment we arrived, then another when we had finished shoeing their three nags. The only trouble was what they served the tea in was a very nice bone china tea set.

Well, this sort of expensive crockery was not a good idea to be placed in my van. As for the little flimsy cups, they only hold a couple of sips for us thirsty guys, and to hold this delicate crockery was not like holding a mug of tea. Our fingers wouldn't fit through the cup handles. We had to use our thumb and a finger to jam the handle between, which in turn made the little finger stick outwards. Another thing was that farriers were not fussy where we dropped the odd hammer or hot horseshoe, but luckily we never managed to cause damage to this expensive crockery, but that nearly changed after we finished the family's horses one day.

My van, a Transit, had a fitted gas forge and an anvil with various tools at the back doors and different size nails and horseshoes on shelves at the side door. This was where the lady of the house would place a tray of her best crockery. After finishing and packing our tools and kit at the back of the van, one of us just slammed the side door shut without checking for teacups. It was a day when we were running a little late, and I suppose it never entered our heads to check for teacups.

Five miles later at our next call, the first thing we saw was a bone china tea set when we opened the side door of the van. A tray of teacups still standing upright on their saucers plus a teapot. Undamaged. What amazed us was how the tea set had stayed upright on the journey. This appointment was down narrow country roads just wide enough for a car, and on a couple of occasions we had to bump the van onto the grass verge when we met oncoming traffic. How we didn't make this expensive set into more pieces, I will never know. It was in the days before mobile phones and we hadn't got the time to go straight back with it. It would have to stay with us until the end of the day. At least the next clients thought it to be amusing. They found a cardboard box and filled it with straw and packed the cups and saucers among it. We hoped it would give it some protection before we could return it, thankfully unbroken.

Sancho

Sancho, a coloured old cob, came into our family lives in early 1978. The old boy was getting on in years with a little arthritis in his back legs but he was still OK to be ridden. I had shod Sancho several times when Isla, his then owner, asked me if I knew anyone who would give a good home to him. She had taken a job in London, and it would be hard to find stables for him and to look after the old boy. She only wanted £50 for him. I thought Judy might like him. At least he wouldn't need a farrier for the next six weeks as I had just got paid from shoeing him. First, I had to find somewhere to keep him although I had a good idea. One of my clients, Mr and Mrs Allan, would take him on as do-it-yourself livery at their yard. After making sure the Allans could take him, I rang Isla back to tell her I had found somewhere to keep Sancho and if I could organise transport, was it alright to pick him up on the following Saturday.

I paid her the £50, and now with Sancho having a good set of shoes on at least I wouldn't be getting nagged by Judy for six weeks. On the Saturday, I had work booked in the morning and had arranged Sancho's transport for one o'clock. I had told Judy to expect me back home about two thirty. She didn't know that I was buying her a horse. I wanted to surprise her and, no, I didn't arrive home at two thirty. Sancho decided he didn't want to go in the horse trailer. We tried everything to get him in that trailer and when we were about to give up, someone had an idea.

'What if we put a bag over his head, covering his eyes so he doesn't see anything?' they shouted.

The idea then was to walk him round in a circle so that he didn't know where he was, then, with straw on the trailer ramp, lead him up into the horse trailer. Why we didn't think of it before I don't know because Sancho walked straight in.

With Sancho safely in his new field, I left for home nearer four o'clock and late. The first thing Judy said as soon as I walked through the door was, 'You're late. We were supposed to be going shopping.'

'I've got you a horse,' I muttered.

'Did you hear me? We were supposed to be going... What did you say? You got me a horse, well where? Can we go and see it now?' she shrieked.

I don't know, the things us blokes do to get out of shopping. We went to see Sancho instead.

Sancho became one of the most faithful old horses I had ever met. We never had to run around a blooming great big field to catch him. One shout, 'Sancho', and he would shout back with a 'whinny' as if to say I'm coming. One or two children and adults were nervous of horses but Sancho had other ideas. He somehow persuaded these nervous people, especially children, that he meant no harm. It was if he was human and so gentle that it was not long before some of the kids were asking could they get on him for a ride.

In 1981 when we bought and moved into our own place 20-odd miles from Sancho's field, we had to find somewhere else for him nearer home. With the house moving and getting my new forge ready, we had not had the chance. We were now paying the Allans full livery to look after the old boy when one day I happened to be shoeing for a young lady called Pat Hinks, and she asked me about Sancho. I told her that we needed to look somewhere nearer home but we had not had the time. Pat had a young horse grazing in her father's four paddocks all on its own. She asked me, 'What about here, Mick. I wouldn't mind an old horse in with my youngster. It'll probably stop charging around with an older mate.'

'Do you mean it? That would be great, Pat, it's costing a fortune paying full livery. Would your father mind?' I asked.

'Well, we will have to ask him, you know what he's like.'

Her father's four paddocks and his large garden with stables attached were immaculate. It was in a beautiful Leicestershire village called Seagrave. He had planted small trees in his paddocks with wooden protection around them to stop Pat's horse from rubbing against them. Mr Hinks, Stanley to his friends, was a semi-retired solicitor who tended to frighten anyone to death even if they were on the same side as him. Once you got to know him, his bite was not as bad as his bark; he was the most helpful and caring person anyone could meet. His house and paddocks had an unobstructed view of open countryside. Both in summer and winter, the scenery was beautiful.

Asking Mr Hinks if we could stable Sancho with him was indeed scary. We had used Pat's horse as the excuse – that our old horse may calm her young one down, and he answered in a gruff voice, 'Yes, I suppose so, but does your horse eat trees? If it does, it will get shot.'

'No, he won't eat trees,' we answered, hoping that he didn't.

Weeks later we learned that Mr Hinks had been working in his garden and left the field gate into his garden open while he emptied rubbish onto his compost heap. Sancho was thinking about walking through into his immaculate garden and stood in the middle of the open gate when Stanley shouted, 'No, Sancho, not through there, good boy.'

And the old horse turns round and walks up to Stanley as if to say, 'I wasn't going anywhere. Got you worried, that'll teach you to leave the gate open.'

From then on, the two of them became the best of mates. Every morning, Stanley went and had his little chat with his new mate Sancho, although perhaps a handful of carrots had something to do with it. One day Pat's young horse flattened one of her father's young planted trees, and she told me she blamed Sancho.

'You didn't, did you? Is he still living?' I asked.

'Oh yes, my father said the old boy is entitled to a tree now and then. That's why I blamed him, my horse would have got shot,' she said laughing.

On our yearly holidays we had to find someone to look after Sancho. Pat would have done it, but with her getting married and leaving home, it was not fair to ask. Judy happened to say to Mr Hinks that we were going to look for someone to look after our horse while we were away.

'What is wrong with me?' he boomed.

She was not expecting him to offer. Since Pat had left, he did have one or two other horses on a do-it-yourself livery basis but didn't get involved with them like he did with Sancho. If they didn't get on with the old horse, they had to leave.

In 1987, poor old Sancho was getting worse with arthritis. He kept getting down and could not get back up due to his arthritic hind legs. We had to lift and help him, and it was getting more often. First it was now and then, but when it got to be several times a day, we thought this is the end. We had to have poor old Sancho put to sleep at 28 years old, but even years later, the memories of that kind old horse live on. Many non-horsey folk knew Sancho through his friendly nature, especially in Seagrave. I don't know how they knew him but I heard that two ladies were chatting on the other side of the hedge of his field when a horse's head appeared over the top. It was if he had come to join in the conversation. I think it hit Stanley more than it did us when we had to have Sancho put to sleep. After all, he saw him more than we did from living on his land. He would miss the morning chats and feeding him carrots every day. On the day the old horse died, Stanley wrote a poem of how he felt about his old friend.

SANCHO

ODE TO SANCHO

On the floor of the barn, his old body lay,
His heart stilled for ever, head on the hay,
The old lungs no longer draw life from the air,
Soft nostrils are still, all matted the hair,
No more to be driven, or ridden, or led,
The sad message is passed, old Sancho is dead.

Five years of his life were spent on my land,
Cropping the grass, feeding out of my hand,
Basking in sunshine, just standing in the rain,
Ah! What would I give to see him again?
Rolling in the snow, defying the wind,
There was never a pony so loyal and kind.

But now he has gone, the old legs are still,
His last race is run, and silenced the shrill,
Call to the mares in the paddock next door,
His welcoming whinny will greet me no more.
I pray that old Sancho looks down from above,
And feels in his heart my message of love.

God bless you, dear Sancho, where ever you are,
Look down on us all from a shining star:
I thank you, dear Sancho, for ever you'll be,
The greatest old pony I ever did see.
J.S. Hinks (Saturday 28 03 1987)

Barefoot trimmers

It is against the law to practise as a farrier where a horse's foot is trimmed ready or for the fitting of a horseshoe without first doing a four-year, four-month apprenticeship and then sitting and passing a stiff examination. Also any farrier can get struck off the register for misconduct or sloppy work. It is not against the law just to trim a hoof without the fitting of a horseshoe. So nowadays there are people in business calling themselves barefoot trimmers or by other exotic names. I am not against some horses going without shoes, but what I can say is I made a lot of money out of one or two of these barefoot trimmers. My other point is if they are that good, what stopped them taking the examination like the rest of us qualified farriers had to?

Although many occasions I have encouraged it if the horse in question is not in work. It is good for the animal to be left unshod if the situation is right. But there is a very big but, not all horses can manage without shoes.

One horse I shod was so flat-footed that it simply couldn't walk around a grass field without shoes. (A flat-footed horse grows its hooves where the toe grows long, and the heel of the foot is short and causes the pressure on the sole of the hoof to touch the ground. In other words, most horse's hooves are concave and a flat-footed one is not.) When I shod this horse, I had to do one front and one hind on one side before I could start on its other side. If all four shoes were taken off, it just couldn't cope standing on its bare feet.

A lady, I will call Margret, who I shod horses for a number of years, was a member of a long-distance riding group. At one of their meetings, they had a guy to give a talk about horses going barefoot. He managed to convince many members including Margret that their horses shouldn't be shod. Of course, any horse owner would be highly delighted with not having to fork out the price of new sets of shoes every six weeks. It didn't surprise me members would be given that information due to the person in question not being a fully qualified farrier. It sounded that the guy giving the lecture did a good job of convincing Margret plus others that their horses didn't need to be shod. Margret's horse was so flat-footed, and when the guy took its shoes off, it was crippled. When she asked how long it would take to get used to no shoes, she was told one week.

Three weeks later, about one o'clock one Sunday afternoon, I got Margret ringing me in a panic. She was stuck in the middle of the countryside and her horse was refusing to move. She was pleading with me to help her. Would I go and shoe her horse there and then. She said she didn't want to listen to a so-called barefoot trimmer again. I think at the time the going rate was about £35 for a full set but she paid me £100 for my troubles, seeing it was a Sunday afternoon. I didn't ask for £100, she told me that's what she would pay me. I wanted to shoe her horse because I wanted to prove a point that when the horse got some new boots on, it would be fine. I knew no qualified farrier would have recommended her horse to go shoeless. Soon others started to ask me if I could shoe their horses as, although not lame, they were not moving freely due to being footsore on the hard, uneven roads and stony tracks they rode on.

GARY POOL

I had known Gary ever since he had started his apprenticeship with my good friend Dave Gully. I had once heard off Dave that another farrier friend had advised him not to take Gary on because he was left-handed.

'You can't teach anyone the trade who's left-handed when you are right-handed, especially forge work,' he was told.

I don't know how true this was but knowing Dave, he may have thought it a new challenge for him. He had had several apprentices who all came out top of the tree. Mind you, I don't think they dared not to with Dave's attitude. He was very particular. Often, I heard him telling his lads, 'It doesn't matter how good you are, there is always room for improvement.'

I think all his apprentices did this throughout their work. Gary being one of them. Dave not only taught Gary how to shoe a horse but taught him to be one of the best forge masters I have ever come across. He could make an amazing set of horseshoes. Some would think, well surely a horseshoe is just a horseshoe, but in the trade there is good and bad. Gary's were well balanced, nicely pitched nail holes for the angle of the horse's foot, and all the things that another farrier would notice.

I don't know how Dave managed to train someone left-handed but thank God he did.

When I started the business with Andy, it was Gary who loaned us an anvil. He would go out of his way to help anyone in need, and years later, he did just that when my marriage to Judy was breaking up. Things were not good at home. I was having to juggle work and look after my youngest son Nick, and I had got work mounting up. Chris, my eldest, 14 years older than Nick, did his best to help me look after him but he worked shifts, and some days it was difficult for him too. Gary asked if there was any way he could help and I answered, 'Yes, come and help me to shoe Martha Cookson's horses; there are loads of them.'

'OK, Mick, when do you want me?' was his reply.

Years later, when things got back to normal, Gary had carried on helping me, especially every other Wednesdays at Martha's. We got into a routine where I would strip the old shoes off the horses and dress the feet, and Gary would follow me fitting. Often, we had three or four or more horses lined up at a time. Once Gary had fitted, I would start nailing on, then he would follow me finishing off.

He too had a wicked sense of humour and in Martha's yard there was no short supply of it. Martha's groom girls could dish it out too, which in turn became a jolly place to work. I remember one time at Martha's, one of her groom girls asked Gary could he show her how to get a horse's shoe off in case of an emergency. He demonstrated on a horse with a smallish foot but got her to try on a horse with shire-like feet. Normally the clenches are tapped back into an upright position and the pincers put beneath foot and shoe. Starting at the back of the foot (the heel) and moving in small grabs towards the toe, pulling the shoe down and forwards. It takes us seconds on a normal foot but on much bigger feet, sometimes we start by pulling each nail out. Gary didn't tell her this when he got her to try on this big-footed horse with shire-like feet with the shoes still nailed firmly on. She tapped the clenches up with no trouble, but pulling the shoe off was a different matter, she couldn't shift it.

Gary kept shouting to her, 'Keep hold, whatever you do, don't let the horse put its foot down.'

Half an hour later, she was still trying to get the shoe off. Still bent double holding the horse's foot and complaining how her back was aching. We both started to laugh and told her to let the foot go, we would do it. When she found out we were taking the P out of her, one could say her language was colourful.

A year or so after helping me, Gary started to have problems with his back due to an unruly horse that had reared up and fallen on him, breaking his pelvis years before. Although his pelvis was fixed, he had complained of back pains ever since and now they were getting worse. He often dosed himself up with strong painkillers just to carry on working. Sometimes his back would go into spasm, preventing him from moving for 10 to 15 minutes. Eventually we put both of our workloads together as he was not comfortable working on his own. He didn't mind the fitting and finishing off but couldn't seem to cope with the pulling off the old shoes, dressing and nailing on.

He was getting worse and walking bent double (at least he was in the right position for shoeing a horse). He had an appointment to see a specialist. He ended up having to spend a couple of days in hospital. I went to visit him one night, and just as I was walking in, I caught him walking out, and wasn't at all surprised where he might be heading. Gary being known to like a Guinness or two said, 'Come on, let's go and get a pint, I've told them am off for a walk due to feeling stiff.'

So into the nearest pub we went, and an hour and a half later and three pints of Guinness in him, we went back to his hospital room. He hadn't told me that he had had nothing to eat due to the hospital wanting to give him a blood test. We had only been back a few minutes when one of the nurses said she had been looking for him and wants his blood. She never asked, and of course he never told her that he was full of Guinness. I think they are still scratching their heads on this blood test. He was amazing, producing pure Guinness. It turned out to be a disc that was causing the trouble and it needed to be tidied up. A 20-minute keyhole operation soon sorted him out. Afterwards, he was bolt upright and we all had forgotten how tall he was.

MARTHA COOKSON'S

At Martha Cookson's stables, I did work every other Wednesday with Gary. I don't know how many horses were stabled at Martha's but there were loads. Some in livery and some of her own which could be hired out for the day. It suited me to have Gary to help me, because there was enough work for two, and if I tried to do the work myself, it meant working a twelve-to-thirteen-hour day.

Martha was a very kind woman, and tea and coffee was never in short supply at her stables. She made an unlimited supply all day. If she was not there, then one of the groom girls would make the drinks, or she just expected Gary or myself to go in her house and do it ourselves. This all worked fine unless Dot, who worked part time, was there. She was a very conscientious lady in her mid-fifties and spoke in a very refined voice. We used to watch our P's and Q's or stop telling dirty jokes if she was in earshot. How wrong we could be, she knew better and dirtier jokes than we did, she could swear like a trooper, and she was nothing like what you expected of her on your first meeting.

The thing that let Dot down most was her tea and coffee making. You wouldn't believe somebody could make tea or coffee that bad. If there was a competition for the worst tea or coffee, Dot would win first prize.

If Martha was out and Dot was there, she would take charge and make the drinks and shout from Martha's kitchen, 'Are you ready for tea or coffee, Mick, Gary?'

'Lovely, Dot, mine is coffee, sugar and milk, Mick's is tea, milk and no sugar,' Gary would reply.

I do not know why we said yes please to Dot to make our drinks, they were just plain awful, but this particular day it was by far the worst. She had a habit of putting the kettle on to boil, then going off and doing other work while waiting for it to boil. The trouble was it was probably 20 minutes or more later when she went back and just poured the now cold water over the tea bags. I mean cold water – even the tea bags shivered.

Dot made tea for me and the groom girls first, whereas Gary was having coffee and she made his coffee separately. When Gary saw our tea, he said he was glad he was having coffee, he didn't like the look of our tea. The tea was horrible, it was cold and stewed. When Dot came out with Gary's coffee, that was something else. The teaspoon looked as if could stand upright in the middle of the mug and the liquid in it didn't look like coffee. When he had sip, I could tell by the look on his face all was not well.

'What's up, Gary, don't you like it?' I said with a laugh.

'Here, have a sip of this, it doesn't taste a bit like coffee.'

'Good God, Gary, you can't drink that. What the hell has she done to make it that bad? l know I can put up with a lot but that takes the biscuit,' I remarked with a rotten taste in my mouth.

Gary thought the best thing to do was throw it away behind my van and out of sight of Dot. He didn't want to say anything as he felt it may offend her, but he was in for another shock, there was a thick black sludge at the bottom of his empty mug, and he got me to have a look.

'What do you make of that, Mick?' says Gary looking green in the face.

'I don't know. I'm glad I had tea, Gary.'

'When she's not about, I am going to blast the mug out with the hosepipe to make it look as if I have drunk it.'

Gary did blast the gunge out of his mug and carried on working when he heard Dot shout from the kitchen window.

'Oh, Gary, what did your coffee taste like, was it alright?'

Gary being polite, replied, 'Lovely, Dot, spot-on, ready for another one soon,' hoping she hadn't seen him throw his coffee down the side of the van.

'Oh thank God for that. For one horrible moment I thought I had used gravy granules,' she shouts.

Martha's stable yard was a pleasure to do work in despite Dot's tea and gravy with sugar and milk. She seemed to appreciate all the hard work and long days we did for her. It was hard work but the atmosphere and the fun made shoeing the horses a lot easier. When the day's work was over, Martha always invited both of us into her kitchen for a 'drink drink' as she put it. The Scotch she put in our glasses was far too generous, especially for the drive home, and she often used to say, 'Would you like dinner as well?'

One day we thought we might have to have dinner with Gary telling Martha's other half Sam he may not have peeled enough potatoes for their evening meal.

It was again after we had finished work and had to go for our usual drink in Martha's kitchen. Sam had a bag of potatoes that would have fed a couple several meals, and he asked Gary, 'Do you think I've peeled enough for four? We have friends in for dinner tonight.'

He'd probably done more than enough, but Gary joked, 'Good God, Sam, I would do that amount for myself.'

Not thinking for a minute that he had taken him seriously and with the grooms now in Martha's kitchen, no one noticed Sam carried on peeling the whole blooming bag of potatoes, until Martha shouted at him, 'Sam, there's only four of us. Why have you done the whole bag?'

'Gary said he would do this amount for himself,' he said, showing the original amount when he had asked Gary.

'Ay, I said I would do that amount for myself, Sam. I didn't say I could eat them all though,' laughs Gary.

That night, we both thought we might have to have dinner with Martha and Sam's guests, with the amount of spuds Sam had prepared. Although shoeing horses gave us both a healthy appetite, I don't think we could have eaten that many potatoes.

One nice sunny spring morning, Gary came to give me a hand to shoe 26 horses. He asked if he could stay the night at my house so we could have an early start. It would give us a chance to get the whole lot shod that day and be able to finish at a reasonable time, instead of seven or eight o'clock in the evening. It made sense for him to stay the night for two reasons. One was to save time for Gary travelling 15 miles from his own house to mine, the other was he was not good at waking up early, but I could soon solve that.

We got to the first call at the crack of dawn with the sun just starting to rise, the air nice and fresh to shoe the first two horses of the day. The vibes we got it was going to be a good day, we both knew it, and the first two horses were perfect and we had them shod in no time at all. The second call, the horse owner couldn't believe he was not the first call of the day when we arrived at just after seven to shoe for his two. Leaving at just gone eight and four horses shod, we were on a roll. Just two calls left, one with fourteen horses and the other with eight, and we were hoping for no hiccups. The lady who ran one of the stables was often never organised and could hold things up, so we made her the last port of call where she had the eight that had been booked in for shoeing.

I can't quite remember exactly what time we got to do the last eight horses but it was sometime middle of the afternoon, and we were both half-expecting she was not going to be organised.

'Start on this one and I'll go and find the others,' she would say and bring one horse.

We didn't want to shoe her horses one at a time. With two of us, we wanted two, three or four all at once, so that we are not standing around watching one another. Soon we were asking for the others due to getting the first one shod. If she had got two ready for us, two takes the same time for us as one when by ourselves. Not only this, stopping and starting knocks us out of our stride. Everything seems to be hard work, especially when the first call was some nine hours before. The woman did start bringing her horses in twos, and about half six in the evening told us we were on the last horses.

I said to Gary, 'We must only be doing seven, I thought there was eight.'

We were nearly finished and both thinking that's it all done and unwinding from a hard day's work when we had to wind ourselves up again. She'd found the eighth. It was the worst feeling in the world to muster the strength to do the last horse. If only she had brought two out when we first got to her, we could have been on our way home instead of looking at each other doing this last one. Somehow having to wind ourselves up, the last one seems to take twice as long as normal and probably does.

With the day being hot and sunny and both of us knackered, we decided a well-deserved pint of Guinness was calling us. The first pub we came to, we were in. When our work boots touched the deep pile carpet and we smelled the aromas of fine diner's food being served, I thought perhaps we should go somewhere else. Gary was first and in and strode straight to the bar and ordered two pints of Guinness. It never entered his head we were not dressed in the right attire for that place. It sold Guinness, and that is all that mattered to him.

The barmaid looked us both up and down while pouring our pints, thinking, *what on earth are those two scruffs doing in here*? Now and then she kept sniffing. Gary asked her if she was coming down with a cold, knowing darn well it was the aromas of burnt horse's hoof that were embedded in our sweaty work clothes.

The first mouthful of our pint was so sweet and by the time the barmaid was giving us our change, Gary was ordering another round. His first pint never touched the sides but I was not sure I wanted another one. All the diners were now staring at us. Were we putting them off their meals through our appearance, or worse could they smell us? Gary was unperturbed, he wanted another pint; it wasn't his problem that we might be putting people off their meal.

We did leave after our second pint and I don't know who was more relieved, me or the pub staff. Although they never asked us to leave, I could sense the relief on their faces when we did. For me, the whole time in there, I couldn't actually enjoy the pint. A more rough and ready place would have suited me better, having been dressed in smelly work clothes.

One spring day when we were shoeing the last horse of the day, I was with Gary at stables where different owners kept their horses. I didn't shoe all of them there but I knew most of the other owners. While I was working on the horse we were shoeing, Gary went to help a young lady tacking her horse up ready for her to ride. She had unhooked the head collar from the horse's head ready to fit the bridle, and before she could loop the rope and head collar back round the horse's neck, it strode forward. Gary saw this and knew her horse was going to try to escape. He rushed to help and got his arms around the animal's neck but the horse had a different idea. It was going to escape no matter what. Gary was clinging to the animal and it was gathering momentum, and so was Gary. Its strides were getting longer and quicker and so were Gary's. He tried to get one hand on the nag's nose to pull its head down and sidewards to stop it charging off, but it was not working. The horse started to quicken its pace even more, so too was Gary. Both were headed for somebody's immaculate allotment that had got rows of glass cold frames covering growing plants.

I was watching with the horse's owner while Gary and the horse careered across this allotment at breakneck speed. I heard the smashing of glass as they went. It didn't make any difference if Gary tried to shorten his stride or lengthen his stride, but his size 10 boots seemed to land straight on top of each cold frame. What amazed us was the horse missed the whole lot and, like Gary said, he couldn't seem to let go. Well he did let go in the end, or rather lost his grip. Then after the horse had its bit of fun, it stopped at the field gate and waited for the owner to come with its head collar.

Luckily the allotment owner was not there, and once my client's horse was shod, we made a quick getaway.

Awkward clients

One of my clients, who I will call Jed, had a bit of success at show jumping with one horse I will call Silver. If the truth were known, it was not so much Jed's riding skills that brought them so much success, but more how good Silver was. Folk had often told me it was more the horse that won competitions than the skill of the rider. In other words, Jed was a one-hit-wonder in the show jumping world. Although he competed on his other horses, he never gained the same success. I had heard stories how good a showjumper Silver was, but this had happened 20-odd years previously and Jed talked to me as if he was still the star of the show jumping circuit.

He liked to think he was above others and everybody should drop everything and be at his beck and call. He tried it with me on several occasions. He often used to ring me late at night to book several horses in for shoeing and expected me to be there first thing the next morning. Time after time, I would try to explain that I had had other work to attend to first as other clients had booked me a week or more in advance.

Jed was not interested and thought his horses were more important than the other owners. It didn't help that he left booking me until his horses were in desperate need. He never thought, and it didn't matter that I wanted a few days' notice before I would be able to visit him. He thought he was far too important and he had got priority over my other clients. Well, even though he gave me a lot of grief, he did pay well and did give me a lot of work.

After several years of doing work for Jed, things came to a head one day. I arrived one morning and found Jed in a foul mood. His girl groom warned me first he was going to have my guts for garters as he wanted me three days ago. Well that was when he phoned me to book an appointment. Not only that, but this poor woman looked at me with a swollen face and could barely see out of one eye. The other was closed because of the swelling. She was black and blue and seemed to be in pain every time she moved.

'What happened to you?' I asked.

It turned out she was helping Jed to clip a difficult horse and he got her to hold the horse's nose in a twitch. The trouble was the animal after a while started to shake its head around. When that happens, it's best to get the twitch off as the animal means it is about to go berserk. It's the same as if it's a human who is desperate to get out of a difficult situation. Jed, instead of been concerned about the girl's injuries, got angry with her for not keeping the nag still. Well, with the best will in the world, that is easier said than done. It doesn't matter how strong a person is, the horse's strength will win every time.

Anyway with the horse shaking its head, the twitch came out of the girl's hand and was swinging around like a helicopter's rotor blades and struck the poor girl in the face. It also struck out and knocked her onto the floor. Jed never asked her if she was alright, he shouted at her that it served her right for letting go of the twitch.

I was really worried about her as she had not been checked out by somebody with medical knowledge. The poor girl lived in Jed's house and in the middle of the countryside. She had no means of getting to a hospital unless Jed took her, but he was in a mood as the horse clip still needed to be finished. That was more important to him.

He certainly looked angry with me when he came storming out of his house with a horse whip in his hand. He was calling me all the names under the sun, and if I didn't jump to him when he wanted me, he would soon sort me out, cracking the whip two or three feet from me.

I don't know who saw red the most, and I said he was going to be in a big mess as he had got to find another farrier, and it's the last time he will have to threaten me with a whip. He was shouting how I can't afford not to do his work, and I soon told him I could and got in my van and drove off.

Later in the evening, I got a phone call, not from Jed but one of his mates, to say he wanted to apologise about his behaviour to me and I could shoe his horses at my convenience? I smelt a rat. Why wasn't Jed ringing me instead of his mate? I knew it was not Jed's way to apologise. He apologised for nothing. He just wanted his horses shod, but with him cracking a horse whip at me, that was the last straw. So I replied that if Jed hadn't got the guts to ring me himself, I didn't want to know. As for the girl groom, I heard she left working for Jed not long after and recovered from her injuries.

Interfering know-alls

In my job, I came across people who wanted to give me advice on how to shoe a difficult horse. This happened to me one day while I was shoeing a pony called Cassie, whose owner was called Josie. Cassie didn't mind me taking off her old shoes as long as I rasped the clenches off instead of using the normal method of a buffer and hammer. (The buffer is chisel-shaped and is used to tap up the nail clench.) Trimming her feet and the smoke from the hooves when fitting the shoes never bothered Cassie. In fact she was good in every way as long as I didn't tap her hooves. This then became impossible when nailing the shoes on. It then became a nightmare with her rearing and kicking and striking out at not only me but anybody nearby. So for our safety, other methods had to be deployed.

I always gave any animal the benefit of the doubt before using drastic measures just in case they had had a change of heart to behave. Again I tried to nail the shoes on Josie's pony and Cassie was not having any of it. So we would revert back to how we did the many shoeings before. The tong handles I used to get the hot shoes out of the van's portable gas forge.

Josie would hold her pony's nose between the handles, and I could nail the shoes on with no more bother. She didn't even have to put much pressure on. Some folk use a twitch.

A twitch is best described as a shortened broom handle with a hole in the end and a loop of string threaded through. The loop is then put over the horse's nose and twisted. I was not overly keen on this method.

Josie was not cruel to her pony but didn't want to see me hurt. We had used this procedure many times before. I could nail the shoes on better and tighter without the fuss from the pony leaping and dancing all over the place and without anybody getting hurt.

One day though we were into our usual routine and I had nearly finished Cassy when a bossy know-it-all horsey woman arrived on the scene. She saw Josie gripping her pony's nose in the tong handles and demanded she remove them immediately. She told us patience and kindness was all that was needed.

I had nearly finished and was nailing on the last shoe, a hind one, when this woman came to interfere. It was impossible to get any further. The nag immediately started to create havoc. The shoe had got two nails in with the sharp ends wrung off to a shorter length. The third nail was in and not wrung off, so had a long, sharp nail end sticking out from the side of its hoof. When the pony is snatching and kicking out and a nail's protruding, it can rip your skin open like a can opener.

I could hold my temper no longer, not because the pony was being a pain, but this woman who thought she knew better. I asked if she could pick the pony's hind leg up.

'Of course I can,' she shouted at me and started to talk to the pony.

She kept on about patience and kindness were the best methods and rubbed her hand along its back, then down its hind leg, saying, 'Come along, darling, show me how clever you are,' and sure enough, she picked the unfinished foot up.

I knew picking the pony's foot up was easy, but to nail it on was a different ball game. So I gave her the hammer and asked her to tap the horseshoe as if she was knocking a nail in. Before she tapped the shoe, I was already wincing, waiting for the accident to happen and boy was I right. After the first tap, she went flying onto the ground. The pony had not only given her a good whack, but the sharp nail had slashed open the palm of her hand. As she picked herself up off the floor, I said to her, 'Come on, let's see you pick its foot up again; after all it's only patience and kindness is needed.'

'It's kicked me and my hand is slashed open,' she cried, now holding a hand full of blood.

I had no sympathy for her, it didn't matter to her if I got hurt instead of the pony. The owner didn't mind us using the tong handles to restrain it. Anything that made the job easier and safer, Josie was all for it. The interfering know-all could see that I was not bothered about her cut hand and was surprised I had asked to pick the pony's hind foot up again.

I believe I said something on the lines, 'We will fix your hand when we have finished, that's what you would have said to me. Are you still using your patience and kindness method? Go on, I dare you to pick its foot up and give the shoe another tap with the hammer. If you dare not, clear off and let us get the job finished.'

She couldn't leave quick enough, and with her gone and the tongs gripping the pony's nose we had it finished in minutes without any sign of misbehaving. I apologised to Josie if I upset her talking to her friend like I did. It turned out this bossy know-it-all was not really her friend anyway and she was pleased it was her who got injured instead of me. She said, 'It served her right, and I was the first person to stand up to her. She is an interfering busybody.'

I think when Josie took the tongs off her pony's nose, she was a little afraid of this woman. On the many appointments after, I never once had the pleasure of meeting this so-called knowledgeable horsewoman again.

TOFFEE-NOSED

When I worked for John, I had a run-in with one of his customers while John was away on holiday. Before he went, he told his clients to ring our house as Judy would take any bookings. I know I was the only one on duty as, if I remember, Mick W was away at college on a farrier course. (Something all apprentices have to do.) John had already got work booked in for me before I left. Everything had gone like clockwork until the Tuesday of the second week. I had only just got home when Judy informed me I was in trouble.

'Why, what have I done wrong?' I asked.

'It's Bill Jones who owns the stud.'

'What about him.'

'He rang about four o'clock to say he got all the mares in ready for you to trim their feet and you didn't turn up.'

'I thought John wrote down Wednesday, it's Tuesday today.'

'He did.'

'Did you tell Bill?'

'Yes.'

'Did he apologise he got the wrong day?'

'No, he didn't, he had a go at me, telling me you are just like John and no effing good, and he bet I was an effing peasant who couldn't read. With a few more fs and bs thrown in to give the sentence more of an essence,' Judy replied.

When I heard he called Judy a peasant who was illiterate, I was on the phone to him straight away. After all, Judy out of the goodness of her heart was only taking bookings and not to be abused by some toffy nose git. This guy had a history of treating women like dirt, and I was not going to let him talk to my wife like that.

When I got hold of him on the phone, I asked in my best telephone voice was I talking to Bill Jones, when I knew damn well it was him. When he said yes in a posh voice, I let him know who he was talking to, and I had something more important to tell him about and it was not his horses. I think the call went something this:

'Bill Jones speaking. How can I help?' (Posh voice.)

'Oh, hello. Mick O'Reardon.' (My best telephone voice.)

'Yes.' (Not so posh.)

(Me.) 'Don't you ever use bad language to my wife ever again. She is not a peasant and can read. In fact she is more educated than you as she would never lower herself to be like you. I once thought you to be a gentleman but obviously I got it wrong, you are just like dirt in the gutter. If it's you who has got the wrong day or John wrote it down wrong in the diary that is between you two. So, in future, less of the bad language to my wife and goodnight. See you tomorrow as originally planned,' and put the phone down.

Next day, when I arrived to trim at the stud, Bill Jones was there waiting. I thought he is going to give me an earful of how I spoke to him. As soon as I got out of the van, he spoke as if nothing had happened. He asked if I would like a drink before I started trimming his horse's feet. I suppose I showed I was still annoyed with him and said, no, let's get the job done. He had never offered before to make a mug of tea for me, in fact I hardly ever saw him on the yard. He just left his grooms to help me.

I knew John was going to be home from his holidays on the Saturday and as soon he was back, he rang me. I had a load of money I had gathered from clients to give to him. I thought I wanted to tell him what happened at Bill Jones before he gave John a different story. John didn't seem too bothered how I had spoken to his client, and I am not sure if he had got grief off him as a few years later, when I was in business, I got a call from Bill Jones asking if I could—! Before he got any further, the answer was no. I have a good memory.

Squealing Mare

One nice summer's morning, I had an appointment to shoe two horses in a paddock in Loughborough. One of the horse's owners, a young girl who I had shod for several times, had asked me if I could shoe a new horse at the same time I attended to hers, which was now in the same field. It belonged to a fourteen-year-old girl.

I agreed to shoe them both at the same time and never thought of asking anything about this horse or its owner. After all, most stand perfect, especially young kid's horses.

I started on this new horse first and it soon became apparent it was no easy task. After a session and a half, I managed to get front shoes on but could I hell get near its back ones. It kicked and squealed when I tried to rub my hand across its back, never mind touching its hind legs. Mind you it squealed whatever part of its body I touched. It was having none of it.

I asked the young girl, 'Is it always like this? What happens when you put the saddle on?'

'We haven't managed it yet, my dad is going to train it,' she remarked.

'Is your dad horsey?' I asked.

'No, he's a stockbroker. He bought it off Jim Perkins, it's called Twizzle, it's been shod before.'

Everything started to make sense, it was true it had been shod before but not lately. My old farrier mate Brian Porter did Jim Perkins' work and I remember him saying about how a vet was called to sedate a horse for him to shoe. In fact nothing had been done to it for months, judging by the state of its feet.

'It's going to take more than us to get hind shoes on and not out here in the middle of a field,' I said to the young lass, meaning it may need tranquilising.

She told me to start her friend's horse and she would go and get her dad. While I was doing the other girl's horse, a guy with a pinstriped suit appears. He told me he was the owner of Twizzle and had come to give me advice on how to pick its hind feet up.

'Oh, how do I do that?' I asked.

'Make a mad grab of its leg and cling on until it gets fed up kicking,' he instructed.

'I have a better idea. You make a mad grab of its hind leg, and I will take over when it's fed up of kicking you,' I snapped.

He didn't seem to like my idea and started to get a bit stroppy with me. I usually got praise off other owners with difficult horses, but the opposite from this know-all. From what I later found out, I did well without it being sedated to get its front shoes on. I was willing to have a go with a vet's help until he told me I was no good at my job. He also told me if I didn't get hind shoes on, he was not going to pay me because I must not know how to handle horses. I did get paid when I threatened to tell all the other farriers what a bastard he and his horse were.

It turned out this bloke knew as much about horses as I did about stockbroking. Jim Perkins must have seen him coming because no one else wanted to touch this horse according to Brian when I asked him later.

Months later, I bumped into the daughter, who told me they were sending the horse to Melton Mowbray horse auction sales as her father was not getting on too well training it. They had to move the horse out of the field at Loughborough because it kicked merry hell out of the other horses and it was now in a field on its own. Also, when could I go to take off the front shoes I got on because no other farriers would touch it? I soon reminded the young lady how her dad told me I was no good at my job when I got the front shoes on their horse, so I can't be any good taking them off.

Common sense

Sometimes, it is hard to believe some owners have no common sense on how to look after their animals. I don't expect owners to know what is wrong if their animal looks under the weather or know why a horse has gone lame suddenly. Perhaps that is for a vet or farriery to find. What I do expect is that owners have feelings for their animals. Whether it be horses, dogs, cats, cattle or whatever, they all have nerve endings and feelings. I know one or two don't mean to be mean through ignorance and a little push in the right direction puts them right. That is fine, but at least they do ask for help. It is the ones who start treating their animals with minerals and supplements themselves because their horses are all lethargic or whatever. Some never in a million years think it might be their own fault how they are treating their pets, and forget they have feelings and need to rest.

A lady who had a Welsh cob that pulled her around the countryside in a trap never for one moment thought it was her who caused her pony to fall onto its knees. She had broken the pony into a trap (cart) herself, and from what I gather, it was good at its job. It behaved itself perfectly no matter if it was to shoe clip or whatever. In fact it was her best friend. There definitely chemistry between them, but I think she forgot her faithful friend needed to have a rest now and then.

She had mentioned to Willy and me about how her pony had started to trip and once fell and took the skin off its knees. It was happening more and more. Our first thought was we would change our shoeing methods and put a slight roll on the toes on her pony's front shoes. We hoped this would make the break over better.

On the next appointment, we were told rolling the toes had not worked. So we tried something else, and after several more shoeings, we were running out of ideas. It was only when I asked what actually happens and when.

As soon as she said, 'It is always when we are on the way home.'

'Are you out driving the pony for long?' we asked.

'Oh yes, we can be out for five or six hours most days.'

There was nothing wrong with the poor thing apart from it was knackered and tired. I think the lady in question would have been falling on her knees if she'd been trotting around the countryside for five or six hours every day pulling a cart. She was not alone in being ignorant that their animals needed to be rested as there were others who would be red-faced if I named them. It didn't occur to these folk that animals can get tired too.

Years ago, another lady client, I will call Debs, had four mules. I had not had a lot to do with mules and always thought mules could be stubborn and awkward by nature. Well, how wrong I could be. Debs was not at all horsey but was persuaded by a friend to foster these animals. She had got a couple of paddocks at her home which a farmer used to put sheep in now and then, and outbuildings converted into stables. I think the RSPCA were involved as they were not in a good state when Debs took them on.

As the months went by, she had got the mules back to better health. They seemed so grateful for their new home. She never had to go running around the field trying to catch them. Once they heard her shout, they would all trot straight away over to her.

As for me, I only went and trimmed their hooves every couple of months. I heard stories how mules could kick and be awkward but not these. Deb would just tie them up to a fence while I trimmed their hooves and she'd go off to make a mug of tea for me. Not once did they misbehave; often they had picked their own leg up ready for me.

One day when I finished trimming the mules' hooves and having a tea break with her, I said, 'That first phone call when you asked me to trim your mules' hooves, I thought this could be hard work, but yours don't act like mules.'

'What do you mean?' she asked.

'Well, I always thought they could be stubborn,'

'Stubborn, what do you mean, Mick?'

'Well, I have often read how pack mules just refuse to budge when working.'

'Do you call that stubborn? Think if you were in their shoes and you were knackered, you would stop and have a rest, wouldn't you. It's the same with a mule once they get tired, they stop, whereas a horse will keep going until it drops.'

'Do you know, Debs, I never thought of it like that.'

I then began to think of that lady's driving pony. If only that pony had been stubborn and refused to budge when it got tired, it would never have fallen and skinned its knees. Deb's mules changed my opinion, perhaps they are the intelligent ones.

THE KITCHEN

One wet Friday afternoon, I had an appointment to shoe a driving pony for a couple I will call Steve and Jenny. They lived on a housing estate on the outskirts of Leicester with two scrap cars parked in their front garden, not to mention other rubbish. The net curtains in the living room windows had changed from white to a dirty brown colour. Steve resembled Onslow from the television show, *Keeping up Appearances*. No matter what the weather, he wore either a tee shirt or vest, a back-to-front hat, and a roll-up was continually dangling from his lips. His wife wouldn't have looked out of place on some seedy nightclub door and resembled Onslow's wife of the same show.

Even though they dressed and looked like some hard nuts, they never showed it to me. I was always welcomed with a mug of tea, and they did anything to help me to make my job easier. Their pony was kept in a field they rented off a farmer behind their house. Even though they had a stable at the bottom of the garden, it was impossible to get my van near. Usually I shod the pony on their driveway between the scrap motors, but this particular Friday it couldn't have rained harder.

I thought it may be best to come back another day when it had stopped raining. Steve was having none of it. He made room in their kitchen and still wanted me to fit the pony's shoes hot. They were not bothered about the stink and smell I would create. So in the kitchen we went with the pony.

I never been in their house before and I soon realised it was not much different to the horse's stable. In fact I think they looked after the pony better than themselves as the stable looked cleaner and tidier than their house. Anyway I was out of the rain.

My other problem was what I did do when I wanted to put the hot horseshoe down when fitting. Steve said I could just put it down on the lino floor, he was not bothered about a few burn marks in it. I must say it's a wonder their house never got burnt down that day as a few times we got to stamp out lino when it caught alight.

Apart from trying to set fire to the kitchen, the old nag needed the loo not just a poo but a wee too. It flooded the place out. Jenny did say the floor needed a wash and, judging by the state of the rest of their home, I don't think she was joking. I thought the horse had saved her a job as she just mopped the wee up. I got the feeling no disinfectant was going to be used when I finished. Her kitchen floor was going to be washed in horse pee.

Anyway I got the job done and paid and wouldn't have been surprised if the floor was left smelling of horse urine and poo. I never found out, though, as although I shod the old pony many times after, I never had to set foot in their kitchen again.

HORSES' WELFARE

Most horses I shod, I never found a problem behaviour-wise. If the horse had been handled from birth, often by the time they are ready to be schooled for riding, the job is made easier for everybody concerned: Vets, horse handlers, and most importantly, in my case, the farrier. Well, it was important to me if the thing was easier to handle and stood still while it was shod. After all, I was only there to put shoes on horses, not to school them. It often made me cross when the owner would say things like:

'I can't pick his feet out, so I have left it for you.'

'The front feet I dare pick up, but I'm not touching the back ones.'

'I can never clean the dirt out of my horse's feet, he won't let me.'

The list of excuses went on and on but more often the problem was not the horse but the owner. How on earth did they think the farrier is going to get a set of shoes on if the owner can't or daren't even pick the dirt out of their horse's hooves! It's not the farrier's job to train their horse. It's the owner's job to teach their animals manners. A horse will beat any human on strength, so it has to be handled from a young foal when we can match their strength. I have witnessed owners not touching foals until they notice the feet are getting long. Then the farrier has an almighty battle to trim the foal's hooves. Once finished, they go off back out in the field and are never touched until the next time when the owners happen to notice the hooves are overgrown again. I started dreading it with these sorts of people when the horse was ready for schooling, ready to ride, and its first set of shoes. Foals need to be handled every day from birth, so they are used to whatever needs to be done to them later on in their life.

Some folk are too soft too with their horses. Let's face it, none of them would risk their necks where half a ton of horse was likely to kick their heads in. I have come across horse owners who wouldn't let the farrier be firm with their animals. Most times it was those so-called do-gooders who nearly always had difficult and badly behaved horses. In cases like these, I must admit I have on occasions lost patience and said things that often resulted in a bit of Charlie's Anglo-Saxon language at their animals. I will give an example of a guy called Dick.

Dick had bought two young Welsh mountain yearlings and called me now and then to trim their feet. Willy was still working for me then and it took all our strength and swear words just to do a foot trim. I was dreading the day when he wanted them shod in two- or three years' time. He was too soft with them. Every day these young animals want handling, not when he felt like it like. If a horse gets it into their head, they can use their strength, and the older the horse gets, they get stronger and their strength will win every time. Dick's ponies were out of control doing just what they wanted, not what he wanted. His schooling only lasted a few minutes before he gave up. He was not firm enough with them. It's no good talking in a soft voice like Dick did.

We caught him on one occasion trying to school one of them saying, 'Come along, darling, it is not nice to kick out at me, and if you carry on kicking out at me, we will finish the training session right now,' and did.

Dick certainly wasn't in charge. Not only were his ponies winning the battle with him but with anyone who needed to attend to them.

While talking about Dick, Willy and I did get a good laugh on a nice hot summer's day at his expense. He was going to catch and bring the ponies into the stable. It was a waste of time trying to trim their hooves out in the field because the ponies got it into their heads that they could drag us or take off round the whole field. So the best option was to get them into a confined space like the stable. Willy and I went with him. One pony was standing next to an old bath full of the ponies' drinking water. Dick liked to give the impression that money was no object to him and hadn't bothered to change out of his tailor-made suit. The pony standing next to the bath must have had an itch on its head and rubbed its head up and down his suit.

He boasted, 'Oh, you want to scratch your head up and down my suit, you do it and I can soon get a new one made, darling.'

Well, what happened next was he soon wanted the suit he was wearing dried quick because he was sitting in a bathtub full of the ponies' drinking water. This one had rubbed too hard and pushed him in.

Both of Dick's ponies did not show any sign of showing that one day someone might be able to ride them. Three years later, their behaviour was worse than ever. By then, Willy had left me to start his own business, and I was dreading Dick helping me to trim their feet. He was an absolute useless horseman, even if he thought himself to be good. One day he mentioned putting shoes on one and said he had decided he would leave it another year as it was so headstrong.

Headstrong, if he waits another year it's going to get even stronger. Oh well, I won't have to worry about the rotten thing for 12 months. What a relief, I thought.

Trouble was the months passed too quickly, and with the animal getting stronger and wiser, I doubted that I would get shoes on it. Drastic action needed to happen if this out-of-control pony was ever going to have shoes on its feet. I decided I didn't want Dick around; he would want to give out orders on how best to go about the job. He was good at this as long it wasn't his head that was getting kicked in. So I had an idea!

I said to Dick, 'You know you are thinking about breaking your pony in yourself. Well if it was mine, I would send it to Tony Grinsdale. His stables are nearby, let him have a go. I wouldn't want to spoil a good-looking pony. Tony gets results nobody else can seem to manage.' I blurted it out, not expecting him to take a blind bit of notice.

Weeks later, late one afternoon, I was shoeing Tony's horses when he asked me to run the rasp round a pony's feet. It was nearly dark and the pony was standing tied up outside.

I took one look at it and shouted, 'Tony, has this thing come from where I think it's come from. I may need you to hold it, it's not easy.'

'Yes, it's come from matey up the road, but it's had a bloody good squaring up since it's been here. You will find a big difference behaviour-wise,' Tony replied.

I couldn't believe it was the same pony; it just stood with no one holding it. Good as gold, and I went round its hooves in no time. Tony also said in about a fortnight's time he would need shoes on and made an appointment. At the next appointment two weeks later, I still couldn't believe that this was the same pony that had come from Dick's yard. I put four shoes on and not a murmur out of it. No one holding or helping, although Tony was nearby just in case. As for the next year, it stayed a year with Tony, and it caused no trouble until one day Tony told me it was going back to Dick's.

My worst fear was it would see Dick and revert back to its old ways, and in three weeks it had. Dick could not see he was the problem. He questioned me, was Tony as good as he was cracked up to be? I know Tony had a fault donating lots of his hard-earned money to the local bookies but in my eyes, he will always be a first-class horseman.

Intelligent animals

Old Ned the cart horse

When I was an apprentice, there was an old farmer who used travel everywhere with Old Ned his faithful old horse pulling him in his cart. He didn't own a car, so he relied on his farmer friends to take him to the cattle market or farming functions. Otherwise Ned and cart were his only means of transport. Everybody knew the old horse, and it didn't need the old guy to show him the direction to the village shop or to shepherd his few sheep and cattle. The trouble with Ned's owner was he could be a nasty old sod and tight with his money. Every morning old Ned would come past the forge, same time, pulling the old codger in the cart. You could set your watch on hearing the clip-clop noise made by Ned's shoes on the road. That was when he had a good set of shoes on his feet. This old horse did lots of road work pulling the old skinflint about in his cart so wore its shoes out quite quickly. When the poor animal's shoes wore away to be non-existent, he then became footsore due to the amount of road work it did barefooted.

We knew the old horse needed shoeing because there was one hell of a commotion when old Ned started turning into the forge yard. The old man would shout and swear and end up getting out of the cart to try and coax the old work horse out of our yard. We often told him it looks as if Ned is ready for some new boots, but that would fall on deaf ears. The old horse seemed to know if it had sore feet, and if it turned in to our place and got new shoes on, he would be more comfortable. This performance often lasted a week or more until the old boy gave in. It's just a pity the owner didn't want to understand the poor old faithful nag was suffering. It was not that he was short of money. When he died, he was one of the richest people in the local graveyard.

NO HEAD COLLAR DONKEY

One evening, Willy was out with his friends at a pub in a little Leicester village. The landlady overheard him telling his mates how busy we had been with work, and she asked what kind of work he did.

'I am an apprentice farrier, learning horseshoeing,' he told her.

'I need a farrier. Would your boss be interested in trimming my donkey's feet?' she asked.

He told her we came to a big stable yard near to her every Friday and was sure we would fit her in. She told him she would keep the donkey in the stable on the Friday and could we call if we had time. Willy mentioned it to me, and we both thought it wouldn't take long to dive in and trim its feet, seeing we were more or less passing her place.

Lunchtime on the Friday, we arrived at her pub to trim her donkey's feet. We couldn't have arrived at a worse time for her but it turned out the best time for us. A big gentlemen's shooting party had descended on her pub and you could say that she was busy.

'The donkey's in the stable on the other side of the road. I'll be over as soon as I can,' she shouted to us.

Over the road we went to find the donkey in its stable with no head collar. We entered the stable to find a donkey with overgrown feet. Willy put one arm around the donkey's neck and gave it reassuring pats with his other arm while I trimmed its hooves. Perfect, the donkey was as good as gold, we wished everything was that easy.

'Why had she let its feet get that long?' I said to Willy.

Back into the pub we went to tell her we had finished and get paid. Her voice changed to, no you haven't, you can't have done it that quick; I am going to inspect it before I pay you.

Neither of us could work out why she had changed from a sweet lady into a right old battle-axe in the time it takes to trim her donkey's feet. Was it her way of getting out of paying? No, we were wrong, just she was startled that we trimmed her pony with no trouble. She saw the big lumps of overgrown hoof clippings on the floor and said, 'By God, how did you do it that quick?'

'Willy just put his arm around its neck and gave one or two reassuring pats. Why?'

Then she told us about 30-odd years of what happened when the farrier trimmed her donkey's hooves.

This old donkey was over 30, and because she had dreaded the performance the old thing caused, she tried to leave it as long as she could. The farrier she had used for 30-odd years had retired and then died not long after. She told us it took him nearly two hours to trim its hooves. (It took us 15 minutes.) She told us that it would either leap in the air, kick out or dive on the floor and tuck all its legs under its body so you couldn't get to trim its feet. Both of us knew the farrier concerned, Artie Beaton. He was a nice old guy with lots of patience.

So why was it a sod with him and not with us? Well, if the landlady had not had a pub full of customers we would, more than likely, have had the same performance as Artie. She would have come with us and put its head collar on, that's the most logical and natural thing to do with horses, ponies and donkeys. We didn't know where to look for the donkey's head collar so never bothered. Willy just put his arm round the donkeys neck, and that's when we realised by accident it didn't like a head collar on. Poor old Artie would turn in his grave knowing that he had battled for the best part of two hours every visit for 30-odd years with that donkey. If he hadn't put a head collar on, the job would have taken him 15 minutes.

After Willy had left me, I used to go into its stable on my own and trim its feet with no one holding it. Wherever it was standing, I could pick its feet up, and it never moved an inch while I was working on it.

Horse sedated itself

Last call one Friday afternoon at four thirty, a young horse was going to have its first set of shoes fitted. Willy was with me and we both knew this youngster well and were not expecting too much trouble. We were prepared for a little bit of coaxing, just like when we trimmed its feet for the first time but after a time we didn't need to as it seemed well behaved. I think the mistake I made was booking this horse in on a Friday afternoon as over the years I found if things didn't go to plan, it always seemed to happen on a Friday afternoon. It either started pouring with rain when halfway through shoeing and caused horses to become impatient. That then that turns into an almighty struggle or it could be one not keen to be shod.

Although that Friday afternoon the weather was a fine summer's day with no rain in sight, we never imagined what was going to happen. The horse's farmer owner was selling the horse and wanted it shod before he put it in the local horse sales. Ann who helped him had got the horse tied to a barn stanchion that housed various bits of farm machinery ready for us. We had shod many of the other horses in the same place without any incident, so we thought this job was going to be no different.

This horse, though, was no problem to trim and fit the shoes. It became a problem when we tried to nail them on. It seemed to know when I was about to drive a horse nail into its hoof and would rear up. After several attempts, Ann tried to coax the youngster with a bucket of feed. That often worked as it took the attention away from what we were trying to do to it. This horse, though, could eat and jump around all at the same time. We tried to restrain it with the tong handles on its nose like a twitch, which didn't work either. We were all thought we may need the services of a vet to administer a sedation injection, but the horse decided to sedate itself.

We had not got one shoe on, and by now it was nearer six o'clock and we were all ready to give up. I thought, *let's give it one more go*, and I went to try to pick its front foot up for what felt like the 57th time. Before I even touched the animal, up in the air it went again. This time it reared higher than the last ones. In mid-air, the animal turned a summersault and fell on its side and walloped its head on a machine that gets potatoes out of the ground. When it got to its feet, it wobbled about like a drunk leaving a pub. I grabbed a foot and in no time at all we had the horse shod.

Two months later, I bumped into another farrier whose client had bought this youngster. He asked, how did I manage to get shoes on it? As although the nag let him remove the old shoes and fit new ones, would it hell let him nail new ones on.

I said, joking, 'Try shoeing it next to a machine that gets potatoes out of the ground.'

Of course he gave me a funny look, as if a machine would calm the animal down. I did own up to him about how it was just a fluke how we managed to get it shod.

Horse didn't like leaving

Over the years, I have found some horses take a liking to some people and not others, like it happened to Paul at Mrs Taylor's. He had no problem with that pony. I have shod horses too where I had no problem, but other farriers had in the past and vice versa. Sometimes it is not the person but the place or stables they are kept at. Years ago, I did lots of work for a horse dealer I will call Alan. One horse came back to his stables three times after he sold it. I had shod this horse many times without any trouble.

Alan would tie any horse I did for him on a nice big concrete base outside the stables. If I needed a hand with anything a bit on the wild side, he was always on hand to help. Most though just stood still and let me get on shoeing them. This horse he sold as good to ride, shoe, box and clip came back to his stables three times for its supposed bad behaviour, it had never once given him or me any grief. In fact, if Alan hadn't been able to find a head collar to tie it up, I think it would still have stood still outside the stable untied while I shod it.

I had seen Alan clipping its coat many times without any trouble and saw no problem advertising it as good to shoe, box and clip. When it got to a new abode it became a monster. The farrier needed it to be sedated to get shoes on. It was the same when it needed to be clipped; as for riding, it was downright dangerous.

Alan couldn't believe what he was hearing. He was sure folk thought he advertised every horse as good to shoe, box and clip like a car dealer just tells customers the good points about a clapped car. I know some horse dealers would sell any horse no matter what. If a customer wanted a horse around eight years old, every nag on the yard would be eight, even though many were often five or six years older. Ageing a horse once it gets past eight makes it more difficult to be more precise.

The trouble was Alan had told the truth about this horse and was beginning to think he was going to have keep it for the rest of its life. His income was from selling horses not keeping them, although he did compete at one or two at shows just to show what potential they had.

The fourth time he sold his horse, he transported it to the new owner's yard and told it to be a good boy and behave. This time the owners thought it was wonderful and never once misbehaved. It was no trouble to shoe, box or clip. It also did well at the dressage that the new owners were into.

I don't think what Alan said was the difference, but more the horse liked its new surroundings.

At another yard where many owners kept their horses on a do-it-yourself livery, there were two stable blocks. There were stables at the bottom of the yard or at the top. If most of the horses I was shoeing were in the top yard, I would park my van there, or vice versa if they mostly were in the bottom one. If odd ones from the other stables wanted new shoes, their owners would bring them to where I was.

A new horse came on the yard and the owner, I will call Joan, asked me if I would shoe it for her. Although Joan's horse was stabled at the bottom yard, she brought it up to the top when I was ready.

It was the last of the day and was a dream to shoe. It had nice round open feet and what I thought was *I would be happy if every horse I shod was this good*. Nobody was needed to hold it and I knew by the first touch the vibes were good.

Six weeks later, Joan's horse was on the list to be shod again at the other end of the yard. The first touch was not good. First it tried running backwards, breaking its head collar. A new head gear was found, but this time Joan held onto it. Her horse was having none of it. She got dragged round the yard. Luckily the farmer who owned the place came to help and after a big struggle we got Joan's horse shod. I couldn't believe how such a docile animal's behaviour could change. When Joan told me she was having issues with it, I thought it was the nag taking advantage of her. It had happened where owners were not firm enough with their animals, but Joan didn't look as if she took any nonsense.

Six weeks later, Joan's horse was ready again to be shod, and she asked if I minded shoeing in the top yard as her horse was as good as gold there the first time. I said I will give it ago. Anything to make the job easier. I was never expecting it was going to happen.

Well it did happen, the horse stood still throughout. No pulls or kicks or rears. I couldn't believe a couple of a hundred or so metres would make a difference.

Eventually Joan swapped stables for one in the top yard, and her horse was as good as gold afterwards. It must not have liked the bottom yard stables.

Late one Wednesday afternoon, six thirty actually, Willy and I had a bright idea of going a little out of our way to shoe a horse that was booked in first thing the next morning. We had decided if we could get this odd horse's shoes on that night, it would free up more time next day to do two extra calls, each having four horses. What we didn't know was that horse was a nasty bleeder. It would kick out at you rather than look at you. Six thirty at night, a quiet horse is hard work never mind a wild one and by God was this one nasty.

Sam Booker had got it in his stables to try to school it for one of his clients. He had warned us it might be a right head case, and when we got there, it was worse than we were expecting and he would hold it for us. We noticed someone had tried to shoe it before us. The job looked a right mess with a front shoe half nailed on. Who was this bodge artist, we thought, but when we had finished, we decided the guy before us had done well to get as far as he did. Perhaps he was not a bad farrier after all.

Before we had got the first foot trimmed and prepared ready for fitting the shoes, Sam had the twitch on it its nose and was using language that was not yet in the English dictionary. It did stand a little better when Sam twitched it and let us get all the shoes fitted, ready to be nailed on. Suddenly without warning, the thing went apeshit. It struck out with its front foot and clobbered Sam on his hip, plus the twitch came off its nose. By now the colour of the stable walls had changed from white to blue with Sam's choice of words. He put the twitch into another use and belted seven bales of shit out of the horse with it and didn't stop for four or five minutes. He didn't care where he hit it, whatever part of its body was in the way of the twitch, it got a walloping. The horse ended up cowering in the corner. When the good hiding stopped, I think the nag, if it could talk, would have been pleading, 'Please don't hit me anymore, I'll behave myself, please, please, please.'

I looked at Willy and we both thought he's going to kill it; I don't fancy nailing the shoes on this thing. God, are we going to be here until midnight. Or worse, it could cause serious injury.

Sam was in a rage, and when he finished giving it a good hiding, he didn't put the twitch back on but shook it next to the horse's head and told it through gritted teeth, 'You move again, I'll blooming kill you, now pick up your blooming feet and let him nail your f***ing shoes on.'

Willy and I believed he might mean what he said and kill it before we had finished, and I do believe the nag thought the same. With Sam still waving the twitch next to its head, it stood perfectly and never moved an inch while I nailed the shoes on.

Afterwards, I said to Sam that was the first time I had ever seen him lose his temper. He was usually such a quiet sort. He told me if you are going to give a horse a good hiding, you give it one, not where owners give them a smack with their hand that doesn't hurt them. A smack is like a good pat which they like. Go for all or nothing, and years later I ended up doing the same thing at another client's. More out of frustration, and I don't think I ever hit a horse so hard ever again.

One of Mrs Dawson's mares had given birth to a foal she called Toffee. It was the first foal that Mrs Dawson had ever bred, and she thought it was wonderful. I was not so sure on visits to trim and shoe her other horses. This foal had a habit of headbutting trees or stone walls for no reason at all from the day it was born.

To trim its feet when it was less than a year old was horrendous. On one occasion it jumped and kicked out, and while I had got hold of its foot, it fell over, taking me with it. A friend of Mrs Dawson's, Bill Saunders, at six foot seven tall and was strong as an ox, jumped across its neck. We had all heard stories that if a horse is on the floor and someone lays across its neck, it's done for. Rubbish, Bill and I were tossed off like a bit of toffee paper. Anyway, one way or another, we did get its feet trimmed that day. It did get a little easier over the next three or four years but one had to be always on your guard. It still tried to kick out if you relaxed for one moment but was handy with its teeth, too, giving a nasty bite. The biggest headache though started when Mrs Dawson wanted shoes on it.

When Toffee needed his first set of shoes on, we felt it would be best if we shod him in his stable. With Mrs Dawson helping me, she said if Toffee was going to be difficult (which I had a good idea he might be), we would just do the front feet.

She told me that Toffee didn't respond to shouting at or violence. After battling with Toffee for an hour, I did manage to nail the front shoes on, but it still needed to be clenched up and finished off. Toffee by now was not responding to anything. Not even a bucket of feed, talking calmly, or Mrs Dawson now using a raised voice and giving Toffee a good clout with her hand. Every time I brought his foot forward to finish off, he would rear in the air. After what felt like the 57th rear, Toffee, this time, caught his unclenched front feet in Mrs Dawson's blouse. She was wearing one of those blouses that were strapless that only covered the top of her arm but not her shoulders. The sharp unclenched nails relieved her of her blouse and bra in one swift swipe.

She looked at me topless with her hands holding the bottom of her back and her bare chest stuck out at me and uttered something like 'Ooh'.

I think I said 'Ooh', too, when she flashed her bare boobs at me, but I think she was in too much pain to be embarrassed. I also noticed where the unclenched nails that had caught her skin had left cut marks that looked worse than being slashed with a Stanley knife.

Mrs Dawson was now in no fit state to help me anymore and staggered back into her house, still topless. The remains of her clothing were still on the stable floor, and I was left with a wild horse to try and finish. I couldn't leave it with all the sharp nails sticking out of the side of its feet. I thought if I could just tap the sharp ends over somehow, it would not be ideal but better than leaving them. When I went to have a go, Toffee had other ideas and had to have a pot shot at me.

Now seeing red, I picked a broom up that was nearby and holding the handle with both hands and calling Toffee by a new name, I was swinging the broom above my head. I too belted seven bales of something out of him in frustration. I had never lost my temper as bad before on any other horse in the years before, and I don't think I ever did again. Never stopping for four or five minutes. Toffee was cowering in a corner by the time I had finished with him. I then pulled his foot forward to finish it off and not a peep out of him. Now should I attempt his hind feet? I thought sod it, I am.

Granted, I cut one or two corners and said one or two unsavoury words to him when I picked the back feet up. I fitted the hind shoes cold and they seemed to go on a lot easier than the front ones. Toffee stood shaking, and all the time I kept telling him the broom was still the corner if he misbehaved.

Meanwhile Mrs Dawson had attended to her injuries. Dressed in her dressing gown, she came back out to see how I had got on and was surprised I had got Toffee's hind shoes on. She wanted to know how I managed, so I told her that he doesn't respond to the nicely, nicely approach, but he did to a blooming good hiding.

A year or so later, the Dawson's employed Reg as their groom and handyman. He hated Toffee. Toffee had kicked and bitten him on several occasions when he was either grooming or putting his saddle and bridle on him, ready for Mrs Dawson to ride. That was the one good thing about Toffee, he was perfect to ride. Reg was now doing all the jobs that Toffee didn't like, and Mrs Dawson was now under the impression he was wonderful. After all, he never put a foot wrong when ridden, the performance was getting his tack on and off before and afterwards. With Reg now employed as the groom, Mrs Dawson never got involved in the looking-after bit of her horses. She just told Reg she would be riding at such and such time, and he would have to start tacking up Toffee an hour before she came to ride him. Her other horses only took a few minutes to get ready, unlike Toffee.

One Monday morning when Toffee was about nine or ten, I arrived at the Dawson's to shoe some of their other horses and was met by Mrs Dawson. The first thing she said to me was, 'Bad news on Saturday, Mick. Toffee dropped dead.'

'What happened?' I asked.

'Heart attack, we think,' she replied.

It was hard to look too concerned with Reg standing five or six feet behind Mrs Dawson but facing me giving the thumbs-up sign and mouthing to me, 'Yes, Toffee's dead.' I must admit it was a relief for me because he had often sunk his teeth into my back and tried to kick me when I was shoeing him too. I had to try my hardest not to laugh or smile with Reg acting like a clown behind her back.

BRIAN PORTER

Brian Porter was a farrier who had a tremendous amount of knowledge in farriery. As I said, he got Andy and myself out of a jam when I couldn't work with psoriasis. I had known Brian for a few years from when we took our farrier exam, and we remained friends until he sadly passed away in 2016. He was a kind man who had lots of what I will call polite cheek. He could say anything cheeky to the ladies, and they would love and laugh and flirt with him. I was sure if I said the same things to them, I would have got a slap in the face.

The day we took our farrier exam, he looked as if nerves didn't affect him; if they did, he didn't show it. He was also a crafty beggar too. We had to do a written theory test, a practical, and at the end, we got asked questions if we had not answered fully on the written paper back then. I not sure if it is the exam format of today, but I am sure it's to a very high standard to gain a pass. Well, the day we sat our examination to become registered farriers, I am sure he left little things out on purpose on his written paper. He knew at the end of the written and practical we would all have to answer orally to anything the examiner saw fit. If any question was not answered fully in the written theory, the examiner would pick on it. Brian knew this, so this is why he left little bits out, knowing the examiner would pick them up. With me, I wrote for England and got asked nothing about any of my answers to my questions. My answers were too fully explained, so I got asked about nerves in the horse's leg instead. I knew hardly anything on this subject, and on advice from a mate's father from my school exam days, if in doubt write or talk a load of codswallop. Surprising how this can work, I don't know if I bored the examiner silly rattling on about nerves I knew very little about or if my theories were right, he never queried me further and I passed the exam.

In the practical part of the exam, though, we had to trim a horse's foot and make a shoe to fit, plus a specimen caulk and wedge hind shoe. (A caulk and wedge shoe is where the heels are raised.) There were 10 farriers and only five forges. So two rounds of about 45 minutes were organised with Brian and myself on the second round. While round one was in progress and we were watching all nervously, Brian strode up to me and said, 'I feel a lot better, Mick.'

'You feel a lot better; my nerves are rattling waiting,' I answered.

'No, Mick, you will feel a lot better; I know we won't be the only bugger who could fail today. Come and have a look at the guy on the end forge; he's awful, we are better than him when we are having a bad day, go and have a butchers,' he said.

'OK, let's have a look.'

He was right, I felt much better too, and he was right, we were not going to be the only ones who could fail either. I would be having the same horse as this guy was working on. He had the near fore; I would have the off fore. I knew I could make my job look better than his, and this probably psyched me up even more for my own turn.

When it was our turn, I was on the end forge and next to me was Brian, and on the other side of Brian was a farrier from the north of England. After we had trimmed the horse's feet, the examiner checked to see how well we had prepared the foot ready for fitting the shoe we were making. In those days a chalk mark was drawn where the foot was not quite level or too long or whatever. The farrier next to Brian asked him why chalk marks had been drawn on his horse's foot, and Brian and myself had none on ours.

'It looks as if they have run out of chalk when they have got to us,' I heard Brian reply.

Out of the ten of us, three failed and seven passed, with one lucky sod named Brian passing with honours. Brian never seemed to be in a rush, he was so laid back he was nearly horizontal. He would plod along at the same pace all day, slow. Well that's what loads of other fellow farriers thought and some horse owners too, but not in my eyes. I suppose I worked at the same pace. One guy at a big livery yard where there were different horse owners who used different farriers said he didn't use Brian and me because his farrier got his horses shod in half the time and was cheaper.

'Does that make us bad farriers because we are too slow?' I asked.

'No, you are just too slow for me,' he answered.

Months later, the same guy came for his usual chat and said, 'Perhaps you were not that slow after all.'

'I thought your chap had got the job done in half the time,' I remarked.

'He's in and out and gone, doesn't have time to listen to my problems like the horse losing shoes not long after he has shod them. I have noticed you and Brian only come back when the horses you do are ready for shoeing. My chap has been back three or four times in six weeks, and charges every visit to knock on lost shoes,' he said.

'He's not that quick then is he if he's got to keep coming back to put his work right, and it sounds dearer too,' I quipped.

I have never rushed to shoe horses. I have always hated it when owners say as soon as I arrived for an appointment that they will have to leave in half an hour, and will I be finished. My reply was, I finish when I finish. It's not that I hang about but I don't cut corners, and Brian was the same. We have both watched other farrier's shoe horses and are amazed how they nailed horseshoes on that didn't fit too well. Brian's favourite phrase was:

'They can't be very busy; they must be looking for something to do next week.' Meaning they would be going back to replace lost shoes.

Brian and I often worked together being duty farriers at three county shows. One of these shows was the City of Leicester show on Abbey Park in Leicester. We would go together in my van even though we both had vehicle passes to enter the showground. The other pass would be given to our wives so they too could park on the showground instead of miles away and also enter free of charge. All the big names in the show jumping world were attracted to this show.

The show organisers really looked after us with a free lunch and tea over the two days it was held, and members' badges for the 'members-only tent'. There was an unlimited supply of tea, coffee and biscuits in a small hospitality room for all stewards, judges, vets, farriers, or anyone else who helps with the running of the equine part of the show. Near to lunchtime, we were allowed two spirit refreshments for ourselves and friends, which one of us had to sign for. So eight of us, which included judges and stewards, used to go together. Which meant in theory we could have 16 glasses of whisky or brandy, with a different person signing after every second drink. Not that we ever got to 16 shots, but one time we all had a little more than our fair share. It was after one session, and I knew we were having a glass too many. I said to Brian, we ought to go and get lunch to sober up a bit. Not that we were blind drunk or anything like that, but let's say if we had a fourth Scotch, words might have been pronounced with the wrong letters. Brian agreed, we would have lunch in case we had the odd lost shoe to knock back on.

One foot inside the lunch marquee, a voice booms out of the public address system:

'Will the farriers please come to the commentary box.'

'Bugger it, someone's lost a blooming shoe, we will have to go, Mick,' says Brian.

'I know, pity we couldn't have had lunch first,' I replied.

Outside the commentary box was a very large lady who was quite a jolly sort and very apologetic for being a nuisance. We both thought this, but didn't say, 'Yes, you are a blooming nuisance. We could have been having our lunch.' She said it was her daughter's horse and it needed a pair of new front shoes. We were only there for emergencies for lost shoes, not for fitting new sets on the showground. Trying to act all professional and polite, the first words that left my mouth sounded to me like, 'You'll ucky to et urs we ust oing for glunch.' Well it sounded like that to me, but Brian assured me I sounded OK. Well, I hope I did. Anyway, who was he to judge? He had drunk the same as me.

Although she must have understood it and said, 'Oh, go and have your lunch. I'll meet you both at your van in an hour, OK? Oh, by the way, the horse doesn't look sound, can't tell which foot it's lame on.'

We both hated this sort of slight lameness, especially when nothing is known about a strange horse. Anyway, we went for lunch. After lunch, the lady arrived with her horse which was only slightly lame. One shoe was still attached to the overgrown foot and we were hoping that was the cause for it to be unsound. It was so embedded in. Brian took the shoe off and trimmed and dressed both overgrown hooves while I heated the new shoes in the gas forge and then fitted. Once fitted, I nailed on, and Brian did the clenches and finished off.

'Trot the horse out, see how it goes now,' I said.

'Sound as a bell,' the large lady shouts, then jokingly asked did we want paying in kind.

We did get paid in money, but when she had gone, Brian said, 'Bloody Nora, Mick, I thought if she meant it, you would have to have her. I'd have the mare; it looked better.'

When doing farrier duty with Brian at the City of Leicester show, he said the same thing when we pulled through the gates of the showground every year.

'Well, Mick, another year gone by quick, I wonder what we will have today.'

He had said the same words all the years I was duty farrier with him. On one occasion, a mate of Brian's was waiting for us at the gate. He wanted us to knock a lost shoe back on, but it was one of his mate's friend's horses. We had to sign in at this show first so Brian would see to the horse with the lost shoe while I would go and get us both signed in.

It was while Brian was bent over, working on his mate's mate's horse's foot, a woman tapped him on the shoulder and asked in a refined type of voice, 'Are you the farrier?'

To which I found out later, he replied, 'No, I'm the carpenter,' and carried on nailing the horse's shoe on.

I didn't know anything about this other horse until about 15 minutes later when I was talking to a steward, when we heard a woman's voice booming out of the public address system. Brian had nailed the lost shoe back on this refined lady's horse, and she had gone back to pay him at one of the ring's commentary boxes. He had gone for a chat with the person who operated this particular commentary box before the show started. He had told the woman where he was going to be as she had to pay him. What he didn't realise was the sound system was switched on, even though nothing had started. The woman apparently was loud without a loudspeaker system, and her voice booms out something like this, and take a deep breath, she never came up for air.

'Do you know you have just put a shoe on Pepper Pot? Pepper Pot won this and won that, its mother was one of the best show jumpers you ever saw, one of Pepper Pot's brothers has done this and that and no horse can beat him and his sister, what a pretty thing mind you the sire was out of a very good breed.'

Brian kept giving grunts now and then with OOO AH, OOO, AH, and when he did get a word in all the showground heard was, 'I think I shod one of Pepper Pot's brothers last week.'

'Oh really, which one, what was it called?' she replied.

'Piss Pot,' he said, and everybody around me burst out laughing.

He had never heard of Pepper Pot or its relations.

New clients, a man and his wife, rang me to see if I would be interested in shoeing their horses. They did a bit of horse dealing and sounded pleasant and chatty. On my first appointment, the husband Bob started to tell me his life story and how he had to do his national service in the army. He mentioned he had met a guy who was in the army called Porter who was a right comedian. Did I know him? He worked with his dad before he had to do his national service as a farrier?

'What do you mean by a comedian?' I queried.

'Oh, one morning we all had to go to the MO for a medical, and when it was Brian's turn, the medical officer asked him if he was run down a bit.'

'What did he say?' I asked.

'Oh no, I came all't way on't bus,' Bob said Brian's answer was, and if anybody knew Brian, one could imagine him saying it.

One night I had a phone call from one of Brian's clients, a lady I will call Angie, who thought Brian was the best thing since sliced bread. Whatever he did or said, she worshipped the ground he walked on. He was her farrier, and none of the rest of us were in the same league as Brian. He could have nailed her horseshoes on upside down, and still none of us would be good enough for her even if ours were the right way up.

Anyway, it caught me by surprise that Angie was asking me to shoe a horse for her. I thought I must be highly honoured to shoe her horses. What have I managed to achieve to be able to do work on this lady's precious animals? No, she soon brought me back down to earth, she was desperate as she had rung Brian and found he was going on holiday the next morning, and he told her to ask me if I could help her out. I must admit, I felt highly honoured to even set foot in her yard, let alone shoe a horse for her.

When I arrived at Angie's, she made me feel welcome and even made me a cup of tea while I worked. She thanked me when I finished and there was no problem with payment. I felt really pleased and thought I must have passed her test with flying colours, being allowed to shoe one of her prized horses. She never gave any hint that she was worried that I may not be up to standard.

Two weeks later when Brian came back from his holiday, he had an appointment to shoe another of

Angie's horses. He had hardly had time to get out of his van before she had got him to inspect my work. Angie was sure something must be wrong with my work but couldn't find fault. She was sure Brian would point my mistakes out to her.

Brian had a puff on his pipe and said, 'The young bugger's shod your horse with two left feet.'

'I knew it, I knew it,' she shouts. 'I knew they must be something wrong.'

'Well, didn't you tell him when he did it?' Brian asks.

'Well, no, I didn't, I didn't want to upset him. What would he have said if I did, Brian?'

'He would have said he shod it with two right ones as well,' he replies with a cheeky giggle.

TEA BREAKS

A client Joan Dixon and her husband lived in a large house in open countryside with a stable yard attached which was surrounded by three or four paddocks. Joan had three horses for me to shoe on six-weekly visits. They were all well behaved and easy to shoe, but with Joan around, it was extra hard work, and *oh boy*, could she talk.

She was quite a nosey sort of person who would like to know all the horsey gossip, thinking I might be the best person to ask. She would stand so close that it was nearly impossible to work. Every time I went to my gas forge or to the anvil to alter a horseshoe while fitting, Joan would be stuck to me like glue. It was all talk, talk, natter, natter. I had no idea what she was saying half the time; next to the gas forge I could never hear a thing. I was probably saying yes when I should have said no, or what or hey. The only time l could get on was when she went to make me a mug of tea, and that was after a lot of hinting.

I would say, 'Look, Joan, I have been here 20 minutes and you have not put the kettle on yet, go and get the tea made so I can crack on.'

'OK, Mick, I'll do that, and I must make a phone call while I make the tea, I won't be long.'

'Good, that will give me at least half an hour,' I used to say in a cheeky sort of way.

Joan knew she talked too much, even her husband used to try to shut her up and she was more of a hindrance to me, and I would want to finish shoeing the horses that day. So if she said she was making a phone call, that was good news to me because it meant some poor unlucky person was going to be stuck on the phone with Joan for the next half hour.

Joan's tea was always hot and freshly made, but it was Earl Grey. I know people like Earl Grey tea but I don't. I used to cringe that I had to drink it; after all, it was me who had got her to make it in the first place. How can anybody drink Earl Grey tea, I don't know, then again everyone has different tastes, obviously it was to Joan and her husband's taste.

I had to force a mug of Earl Grey down my throat three times a visit every six weeks, one for every horse I shod, and after going for three years, she came out with the tea one day and said, 'Well, Mick, that is the last of the Earl Grey and seeing that you are the only one drinking it, we will have to get some more in.'

I couldn't believe what I had just heard, they didn't drink the stuff either. That meant I had forced down my throat over 70 mugs of Earl Grey tea because I thought that was what they liked, and now I found that they had it in and thought we will give it to Mick, he seems to like it.

Over 40 years ago when I was in business with Andy, one of our clients, the Swales family, we had to call them the Hillbillies. That was because they resembled the 1960s *Hillbillies* television show. These Swales could have done the television show of the same name and, by God, were they eccentric. A television company wouldn't have had to hire actors or script writers, all they would have to do was to turn up and start filming at the Swales. It was a different episode every visit.

The Swales family consisted of mother, father, and their offspring, Les. Les was a big, tough-looking bouncer type who you definitely wouldn't want to upset. It was only after several visits when our apprentice Paul went to the shed to get the head collar for the horse when Mr Swales shouts to him, 'Hey! Can't go in there, dawter in't baff.' (Daughter in the bath.)

That is when we discovered Les was a woman. She was having a bath in the shed as the house did not have a bathroom or running water. The water supply was 40-gallon oil drums dotted around their house to catch rainwater. Lighting was gas lamps and candles; cooking was on a big open fire with an oven built in at the side of it.

Mr Swales was a colourful character, with his trousers that finished six inches above his boots showing his brightly coloured red, blue, yellow, or green socks. Sometimes he wore odd socks! His braces kept the waist of his trousers pulled up to his chest, and he wore a trilby hat which looked a size too big on his head.

Mrs Swales was a small-framed lady who walked with a bit of a stoop. She was as tough as old boots, though, and gave the impression she could be the boss of the family. The brown coloured flowery-type dress looked to be the only one she had as she wore it all the time. Also the same went for the white pinny that had seen better days. Her footwear was carpet slippers, and by the look of them, her only pair. Her hair was combed into a bun on top of her head.

The old horse was friendly, well behaved and good to shoe. It was while we were shoeing the horse, Mrs Swales didn't ask but growled, 'Want tea?'

We thanked her in a trembling voice that we would love to have a cup of her tea. That was until Paul and I saw her filling the kettle from a dirty old oil drum with no lid on, with leaves and all the rest of the dirty elements blown in. What was the tea going to taste like? Will it taste oily? We had not got round to mention it to Andy where the tea water had come from as he was dressing the horse hooves ready for me to fit its shoes.

Mrs Swales made the tea with a thin layer of oil floating on top, plus her homemade biscuits. Andy was now waiting for me while I fitted the horse's shoes, and he started to drink his tea. With my head down working on the horse, all I heard from Andy was ergh and him spitting oily tea out of his mouth.

'The tea's got something floating on top, it tastes funny. What's yours like, Paul?' Andy asks, still trying to spit the horrible taste out of his mouth.

'I'm not drinking that; we saw her get the water out of that old oil drum, Andy. By the way, have you tried the biscuits? They are like concrete and need dunking in the tea for a fortnight,' replies Paul.

Yes, three cups of oily tea were discreetly thrown away, and we had to lie about how nice the biscuits we hadn't eaten were. Even their dog was not interested, it had a sniff and walked away as if to say, 'I'm not eating that.' Every visit after that we used the same excuse.

'We had one at every call so far today, tea will be coming out of our ears if we have any more,' would be our reply.

At Mrs Summerton's, though, things were worse than the Hillbillies. At least their horse was good to shoe and inside their house was clean. Mrs Summerton's horses were a nightmare. I had Paul with me on the first visit, and did we struggle. The horses were knee-deep in deep litter, not well behaved, and luckily just needed their hooves trimmed. I know farms can't avoid mud, but hers was one of the worst. The buildings were all ramshackle, with heaps of scrap and broken, worn-out machinery, plus other rubbish filled her farmyard. Not to mention the many rats which were regularly seen scurrying about the place. Her horses were not the best behaved. She kept breeding thoroughbreds, hoping to make them into top-class racehorses one day. None ever made it due to the fact they never got to see a trainer. She did nothing with them, they just ran wild until she was scared of them. On every visit she used to tell us she would have to send them to a trainer, but never did.

Yes, her horses were blooming hard work, often a vet had to be called to sedate the really wild ones, and my God, could we sweat, it would be dripping off us. She offered us refreshments on our first visit, but never again. Her house made any teenager's bedroom look all neat and tidy. At least they wouldn't have had dog muck scattered all over the floor. Old newspapers with God knows what other rubbish were scattered under the kitchen table and over the sitting room floor. Thick dust and dirt covered the cupboards and kitchen work surfaces. The floor, well you kept your boots on and wiped your feet on the way out, it was filthy. I don't know when the tiled floor last saw a brush and dustpan, it certainly hadn't seen a mop and bucket for years. Dirty pots and pans were scattered all over the kitchen worktops, never mind the sink, you couldn't see it. It was stacked sky-high with what looked like three months of dirty pots. There were probably no pots left in the cupboards.

On entering Mrs Summerton's house, the stench hit you. The six Alsatians dogs that never went out, judging by the amount of dog muck on the floors, had a lot to do with it. When she made our tea, our mugs were found amongst the three months washing up in the sink, a quick splash under the tap and half a mug of tea. I say half a mug because of all the sludge still attached to the sides and bottom of the mugs. When she left the kitchen to find her cheque book to pay me, our tea was quickly poured into a pot plant that looked as if it needed it more than us.

After several visits to Mrs Summerton's, one of the lads commented it was a good place to get flea bites or whatever other creepy crawlies that lived in the dirty stables and crew yards. Although we never did get bitten by any creepy crawlies, I had to think about it while having my hair cut one day. I had called at a barber friend called Ian after one of Mrs Summerton's visits. Sitting in the barber's chair, I started to think what one of the lads once said about fleas. An itch suddenly appeared in the middle of my head and got worse where a good scratch would not be out of order. Then it's, *Oh God, can the hairdresser see creepy crawlies in my hair?* Of course, Ian didn't see any creepy crawlies. Although, when I mentioned it to him years later, he said, 'Now you have mentioned it – *well!*' I hope he was joking.

Another thing with Mrs Summerton was often of her cheques bounced. Although she did pay me in the end, I must say she tried one day writing a cheque out for more than I wanted. What was supposed to happen then was for me to give her change in cash. I am not talking of five or ten pounds but two hundred. Alarm bells rang in my head as this cheque was a replacement for the one before which bounced. She took offence when I said I was not going to give her change in cash. I just wanted her to give me what she owed me. After all if this next cheque bounced, she would have got away with my fee plus another 200 pounds of my money. Needless to say she was not happy when I didn't agree to her arrangement.

Reluctantly, she did give me another cheque for the right money, and this time it was honoured by the bank. I thought it best she found somebody else to attend to her wild horses before she did owe me money. Her horses were too much like hard work to work for nothing.

Friendly banter

I like to think that I and the lads who worked for me were never rude, but we often pulled some of our customers' legs with friendly banter over trivial problems. Although it could be cheeky, I liked to think it was more polite cheek. I remember one morning two teenaged girls fell for one of Willy's jokey demon farrier ruses. It was nice spring day, the sun was shining, the birds were singing, and it felt wonderful to be working outside.

These two girls kept their horses in a field in the middle of the countryside with a small stable yard attached. We had shod their horses many times when on this particular day one girl asked Willy, 'Why has my horse got white streaks in its black hooves?'

'Bloody hell, you have to find them,' says Willy

'Find what?' the girl asked.

'Yeah, you've got to find them, it's usually in cattle but it looks as if your horse has got them,' a concerned-looking Willy said.

'Got what?' she asks.

'I bet in this paddock, you will only find a dozen or so,' he replied.

'Find what, Willy? Stop keeping me in suspense.'

'Yeah, you've got to look really hard to find them. As I say, there will only be about a dozen or so.'

'Willy, I will kill you, just blooming tell me, find what?' the teenager screamed.

'Worms,' replied a serious-looking Willy.

'Worms, what sort of worms?' she shouted.

'Little orange ones, they glow especially in the dark; you've probably never noticed them in daylight, they are only half an inch long if that,' he replied.

'What do they do to my horse's feet then, Willy?'

'Well, when your horse treads on them, they stick to the bottom of its foot and suck the colouring out.'

'Really?' she asks.

'Yeah, when we have gone, both of you have a good look.'

When we finished shoeing their horses and were travelling to our next call, we both couldn't believe that she didn't twig that Willy was pulling her leg. A couple of hours later, we came past the two girls' field, and what did we see? Both of them were walking in straight lines, head down, up and down the field, looking for little glowing orange worms. Every visit, they said they had not seen any, and I suppose we strung it out for six months. Eventually, Willy did tell them the truth. By the look on their faces, I thought, *Willy, you could end up with a squeaky voice when they finish with you.*

There was nothing wrong with the horse's hooves. Some are black with white streaks, some are white with black streaks, and some are just plain black or white.

Prices and payment

One lady client owned three horses and couldn't really afford the upkeep on one. My visits were when the horses were weeks overdue, and it seemed to be my fault that I charged money to shoe them. She often tried to knock me down in price, saying how expensive it was to keep three horses. I would tell her I have three kids; it is just the same. At the weekly shop at Tesco's, they didn't want to give me a discount either when I explained how expensive it was to raise three children. My attitude is: don't have three horses, they are an expensive luxury. The easy bit of owning a horse is saving up to buy it, the expense of the upkeep is harder when you own one. The same with children, it can become good expensive fun nine months before they are born.

Inside my van, I had two notices. One said: USE MY EASY CREDIT PLAN 100% DOWN AND NOTHING TO PAY EACH MONTH. The other: THE BANK MANAGER DOESN'T SHOE HORSES, I DON'T GIVE LOANS. This was in 1984 when I was owed loads of money off different stables. I decided that I was not going to do any more monthly accounts, it was payment as soon as I finished shoeing the horses. One or two of my farriery friends said it wouldn't work. I thought *It does at Tesco's when I buy my weekly groceries, they don't give monthly accounts, and what's stopping it working for me*? I was in a position where I could pick and choose which clients I wanted. I had customers on a waiting list.

Not only did it save time and expense every month, I figured I could be more in control of any bouncing cheques. (Which one or two did.) I reckoned that a smaller amount was easier to pay on the day than a month's work of 20 or 30 horses, especially at the larger stables. If the accounts were monthly, some places tried to leave paying near to the end of the second month. So, in effect, they got two months' horseshoeing out of me. Longer if their cheque was going to bounce. The other reason was my money could be sitting in my bank instead of someone else's making interest for me instead. It was one stables that convinced me that was going to be my terms of business.

One big stables run by a husband and wife owed me £850 pounds in the early 80s, and they kept giving me £100 cheques to keep me happy and to buy more time. Unfortunately these £100 cheques kept bouncing. Four bouncing cheques later I told this client I needed to be paid in cash the full amount plus bank charges on my next visit. They promised it would be no problem and would pay me what they owed in full. On my next visit I was hoping to leave with a pocket full of cash; I left with another £100 cheque and a promise the cash would be there in one week's time when I had to shoe the wife's two expensive show jumping horses. They sweet-talked me into taking another cheque, which

I suppose felt better than nothing. The following weekend it was Easter, and I was supposed to go to shoe their two show jumpers on Good Friday, ready for leaving for the shows on Easter Saturday. The day before I was supposed to go to shoe this couple's show jumpers, the bank returned the £100 cheque with *refer to drawer*. I made up my mind there and then I was not going to turn up for the appointment. I did not even ring them to cancel. I knew the horses were desperate for new shoes, and it would give these owners a big problem if I didn't show up.

Having decided I was not shoeing their horses, my phone rang, and it was a booking for three ponies belonging to three young girls. These ponies were all stabled at the same stables and when was the earliest I could shoe them.

'Tomorrow,' I said, being cross with the show jumping people.

The next day was Good Friday. I did the three young girls' ponies instead of the show jumpers and got paid when I had finished. I never gave the show jumpers another thought until early evening when the phone rang. It was the woman asking why I had not turned up. Had I forgotten her, or run out of time, or was I going to shoe them on the Saturday morning before they left for the show.

'No, I didn't forget and, no, I was not going on the Saturday morning. I was so mad that you bounced yet another cheque. I went and shod three young girls' ponies instead. What was the point of doing more work when £100 cheques bounce when you owe £850 plus?' I said.

'It was more important to have our expensive show horse shod than the young girls' scruffy ponies,' she replied.

'Not in my eyes. The scruffy ponies pay better,' I replied.

'Well, it is important you come tomorrow,' she said.

Not wanting to put them off because of the amount of money owed to me, I told her that the only way I would shoe their horses the next morning was if I get paid that night. I would want the full amount plus bank charges in cash, then I would consider shoeing their horses.

An hour later, they arrived with the £850 in cash, and the wife still ranting how unreasonable I was being.

The husband kept saying in a nervous voice, 'Err, slight misunderstanding, we always intended to pay,' and counted out £850 in cash.

I felt a bit peeved he had not added on what the bank charged me for his bounced cheques but not wanting to upset them, I waited until the money was safely in my wallet. Not getting the bank charges had annoyed me and the wife never stopped giving me earache on how unreasonable I was being. I decided there and then never to work for them ever again. I only got what I was owed because they were desperate to have their horses shod. If they had not been desperate, I doubt if I would have got paid, so I told them with a couple of words her husband used.

'Err, slight misunderstanding, I am not shoeing your horses ever again, your wife has never stopped telling me how unreasonable I am. I will never be unreasonable to you ever again, and you won't have to pay me ever again,' I said, in a not-so-nervous tone of voice.

They left arguing, with him telling her she should have kept her big mouth shut, who will shoe them now at such short notice.

There was an awful lot of work at this couple's stables but working for nothing was something I didn't want to do. With a list of potential clients wanting to be on my books and being paid most of the money I was owed, I thought it best to cut my losses over the bank charges and drop this couple's stables before another £850 was owing.

I have always said there are two types of millionaires, one who has worked hard for their money, and one who has inherited and never done a day's work in their life. The ones that made their own wealth, I never had problems with. They seemed to appreciate a good job and payment was never a problem. They understood the traumas and headaches trying to make a living out of a small business, they understood from once being in the same situations themselves. I had the biggest trouble with the wealthy ones who had inherited their fortune and never done a day's work in their life. Or the ones that pretended to be wealthy and lived robbing Paul to pay Peter. It didn't seem to occur to a lot of these people that payment was required after I had shod their horses.

One who pretended to be wealthy, who had God knows how many horses scattered around his stables and fields, rang me to shoe his horses. I had heard from other farriers and various tradesmen about this guy, how it was difficult to get money out of him. On my first visit before I had started the first horse, he told me his terms of business. He said he only paid his accounts every three months, so only invoice him every three months. What he tried to say was to invoice him every three months, and he will try to pay after four months.

I said, 'You have told me your terms of business. Now I will tell you mine.'

He looked shocked when my terms were that he paid when I had finished. It was as if paying me was unimportant. He then said to me in a stern voice as if he was annoyed with me, 'Do you know who I am?'

'Yes, I know who you are. Why? Have you forgotten who you are?' I said.

I was not going to be intimidated by him, I got the impression I might be now intimidating him. I was in a position where I could choose my clients and didn't need the aggro of someone who wanted to leave payment for as long as possible. He then said the wrong thing to me.

'What if I don't pay you there and then?' he said, all cocky.

'Then you had better pay me in cash before I start,' I told him.

'I will have to go to a bank for the cash,' he replied.

'That's OK by me, I will nip off and shoe another client's horse and will come back and do yours when you have got cash,' I said in the stern type of voice like how he had spoken to me earlier.

For the next three to four years, I got paid before I did any work. He didn't like it, but – Oh, well – I did.

While shoeing this guy's horses, I got talking to his groom who said he had to beg for his wages. He didn't pay his other workers on time either.

'Why don't you turn up for work and tell him you will not lift a finger until you have been paid in full?' I asked.

'He will get someone else,' the groom replied.

'Who? I can't see anybody working for him. Too many people know he doesn't pay,' I commented.

I don't know if the groom got paid or not because he left soon afterwards and was replaced by several different grooms who never stayed long. All I know was I got paid before I started, and now and then he would have a grumble how inconvenient it was for him having to make journeys to the bank. It would have been more of an inconvenience to me if he didn't pay me.

Three or four years later, his mansion and stables went on the market, and there were no horses for me to shoe. The horses had all being sold off. He had financial difficulties. That was the reason he was a bad payer; he was only pretending to be rich. He owed thousands to different tradesmen but nothing to me. I never once gave in to my inconvenient ways for him. If I had, I might have fallen victim to him too.

THE FARMER

One night a farmer rang me to say his young son's pony had lost a shoe. Didn't Willy and I put it on properly the last time? I thought he was having a little joking banter and said we would be there on the Wednesday to shoe it. I didn't take too much notice about the lost shoe because he had a habit of leaving them until they were way overdue. Six weeks is the normal time for a horse to be shod, give and take, some will go a little longer and some shorter. It all depends on what work the horse is doing and the condition of the horse's feet and of its make-up. It is not a matter of leaving the shoes on until they fall off. It is the hooves that need to be trimmed. The only way I could ever explain it to these sorts of clients was: Imagine your own shoes having no heels on them, and your toe end of your foot is raised and try to walk. It will hurt and stretch the tendons in the back of your leg. A similar thing is happening to your horse, and he can't take his shoes off on a night. The horse's foot grows down and forward.

This guy I will call Charlie was a bit of a know-all, and his pony had not been ridden for the last seven months, which was his excuse for not having it shod. I wasn't surprised a shoe had just fallen after such a long time. It's a wonder it still had its other three shoes still on.

He had also told me he had bought a thoroughbred, and could I shoe this horse at the same time as the pony. Willy at the time had started to fit shoes and nail on with me watching. If the shoes are not worn out, we would refit to save money for the owner, and we both had a good idea this pony's shoes would most likely look brand new. I said to Willy, 'You do the pony, you've got to start sometime, he's found the lost shoe and I know they will refit. I will do the thoroughbred.'

When we started shoeing, this right Charlie started to have his moan on how the pony hadn't being ridden and not only had it cast a shoe but three months ago started tripping. I still thought he was having a bit of friendly banter until I said to Willy, 'I bet it was your fault it lost its shoe last time, Willy. I bet you didn't clench it up properly.'

Willy, too, thinking it was jokey banter, replied, 'I'll pay attention this time, Mick.'

To which Mr know-all started poking me on the shoulder in an aggressive manner and said, 'Too right you will pay attention, I am telling you, this pony has not been ridden or been out of this field for seven months and now it's falling over.'

When I realised he was serious and didn't understand that his pony still needed to have its feet trimmed, ridden or not, I said in a stroppy toned voice, 'God, am I a bit thick here? I didn't realise a pony's foot stopped growing while you were not riding it. Have you ever thought that is why it is tripping? Its toes are too long.'

Not saying another word, he cleared off and left Willy and me to get on with the shoeing. Willy said to me, 'You know, Mick, you made him look a berk.

I thought he was only having a laugh until he started poking you in the shoulder, trying to blame us.'

'I too thought he was mucking about too until he had a go,' I replied.

We got the shoes on, and I inspected Willy's first shoeing job on his own. His first attempt was OK but not if it was somebody's best show jumper. I pointed this and that was wrong and could lead to the pony ripping its shoes off. Willy said what did I want him to do? 'Take them off and start again?'

'No, leave them, it's not going to harm the pony. It will probably do the pony a favour. I know he'll leave its shoes on too long. Perhaps if its shoes fall off before the feet get too long, he'll have us back sooner rather than later,' I answered.

That was our plan, but plans can go wrong. Four months later, Charlie rang to say the pony needed some surgical shoes as it was walking on its heels and can't put its toe to the floor. Also it was struggling to walk. I had a good idea that a bloody good foot trim and to leave its shoes off may do the job. I had a feeling it had got too fat and developed laminitis from having no work and grazing on lush pasture. It didn't need shoes just to walk around the field. Neither of us could believe Willy's shoes had stayed on. We were certain they would fall off for the animal's sake and didn't. Charlie was the type of guy who wouldn't take advice, nothing was ever his fault and, anyway, what did we know.

When I came across these types of people and it was plain cruelty to animals, I would try my best to help them and push them in the right direction. Most folk do take advice but we both knew what Charlie was like, and both of us used a bit more of a forcible way. The poor thing now needed help from a vet. We both decided that if we ever saw it in that state again, we would have no hesitation but to get the RSPCA involved. Was he going to get the vet in was another thing, and when he told us he would treat it himself, we were certain that the animal was going to suffer more.

When we left, Willy told me he knew an RSPCA inspector, and we both agreed it might be a good idea to get him to give Charlie a call. They did pay him a visit and read the riot act to him, and I had a good idea this right know-all may never have me shoe his horses again. I just hoped that the pony got a better life afterwards.

While I was doing work at a big riding school, lots of their clients used to chat to me while I shod the school's many horses. One middle-aged guy, Sam, came two or three times a week to have a hack out on his favourite nag. I thought it was his own horse in livery at the stables until he told me that it belonged to the riding school. He had taken up riding late in life and had only ridden this one horse. He admitted he didn't know how to tack one up or what or how to look after them. The staff at the riding school had attended to this before he arrived. He also told me he was thinking of buying his own horse and keeping it at his home. First, he was going to have a crash course of how to put the saddle and bridle on and learn all about what to feed it and all the do's and don'ts.

I admired him for learning all the basic needs about owning a horse and not jumping straight in and hoping for the best like lots of others. He knew that the expense of keeping one came after he had bought it. He had his own successful business, and by the sound of him, money was no problem and he was no mug... Well, that was what I thought!

Six months later, he rang me to say he was the proud owner of his new horse called Drizzle. When could I put a set of shoes on? Drizzle was seven years old and he had bought him unshod.

An appointment was arranged and I was most impressed with Sam's super stable block he had built. It had plenty of clean hardstanding inside and out, which us farriers like. Tea and biscuits were brought out by his wife. She said she didn't have much to do with the horses, they frightened her.

'No need to be frightened of Drizzle, he's perfect and very friendly,' I told her.

'Sam says the same, but no, I am not going near,' she replied.

'I must say you and Sam certainly done your homework with the stable design. You have thought of everything, even the most important thing any farrier needs,' I remarked.

'What's that?' asked Sam

'Tea and biscuits,' I said with a grin.

Yes, Sam had pulled all the stops out, he had listened to all advice of the riding school and various other reputable horsey people, but there was one thing we had all forgotten to tell him. Horses need shoeing every six weeks.

I had not heard or seen Sam since I had shod his horse months previously. The riding school had heard one or two reports that he was getting on OK and Drizzle was perfect in every way. I had started to think that he may have got someone else in until he rang me one night to say my work was not good.

'I am sorry my work is not up to scratch, but please tell me in what way?' I asked.

'Drizzle's only seven years old and a shoe has fallen off already,' he shouts.

'Are they the same shoes I put on?' I asked, thinking he must have had someone else by now.

'Course they are, I have had no one else. As I say, Drizzle is only seven and lost a shoe already. He's got years left in him,' he rages.

'I see the problem, Sam. Has no one told you horses need shoeing every six weeks? Your horse has had his shoes on months. I bet his feet are overgrown, Sam.'

'Oh no, don't say. I feel a prat now. I thought once the horse was shod, that was it for the rest of its life. When can you come? Sorry, sorry, sorry.'

This wasn't the case of neglect; it was what he didn't know and only needed pushing in the right direction.

Foot and mouth

I have known foot and mouth strike three times through my working life. The first time was while working at Derek's back in the 1960s, which affected him. Farmers stopped ordering new cattle pens and gates for their farms. They only wanted the bare minimum of people visiting their farms to minimalise infection. It also snowballed into the horseshoeing if horses were stabled on a dairy farm. Horses don't have a problem with foot and mouth, but farmers were more worried about the spread of infection off anyone's clothing, infected footwear, or from vehicles. If we did have to go to one of those farms that had a prized dairy herd or sheep, a disinfected foot bath to wash our boots was at the entrance of the farm. Disinfected straw was scattered across farm entrances to clean any bacteria on vehicle tyres. In later years, a spray to disinfect the wheels and wheel arches of the van was used at many farms.

Although not all stables were affected, it did hit one or two farriers more than others. The last outbreak in 2001, it didn't really affect me but it did my good mate Dave Gulley. He told me he might have to lay one of his lads off. Matt who had just qualified as a farrier was the one in question. I asked him how many days he could give him work for because I could help out and employ him for a couple of days a week. Other days I would get

Matt or Dave's other apprentices to make horseshoes for me instead of me using ready-made's.

Between us we managed to keep Matt in a job, and after the foot and mouth was eradicated, he let me have a loan of one of his other lads if I had a busy day. I enjoy helping other farriers out when they are having a difficult time through no fault of their own.

I often thought one day it could be me who was in need, and I know I could count on Dave, Brian, Gary, and Andy, and many other farriers who would do the same for me.

Young farriers starting their own business

A family I used to shoe for had three sons, and I knew one day two of the sons wanted to become farriers. They lived on a small farm near to me, which had a forge. The eldest son Andrew was doing his farrier apprenticeship near Stoke-on-Trent. On weekends or holidays, he would make horseshoes for me to boost his apprentice wages. It was in the days when I made all the horseshoes from scratch, and even though I had Willy and Paul working for me, we could never make enough. I would have steel chopped to different lengths ready for Andrew to pick up on a Friday night and he would deliver them back to me on Sunday afternoon, made into first-class horseshoes.

A couple of years later when he was on holiday from his job, he would give me a hand with the shoeing of the horses. By then, Willy and Paul had left to start their own enterprises and I often appreciated extra help.

I remember one call we did when Andrew helped me out. It was a bitterly cold winter's day at one of my customers, a husband, his wife and daughter had five horses to shoe. The trouble was the wife made us a very nice coffee every time we got a horse shod. Well, we were grateful of the coffee but each mugful was laced with a generous portion of whisky.

Five horses later, Andrew commented he had never got drunk on coffee before and to be honest I think that customer would have succeeded if they had had six horses to shoe. Mind you, the colder the day got we never noticed.

When Andrew started his own business, I was having to take time off work again to go for a fourth treatment at the Dead Sea for psoriasis. Although he got a little round built up, he was still on the lookout for more. I asked him if he could look after my customers while I was away and I think he appreciated the extra work. He did me proud, and I can remember another time when I had a very difficult horse to shoe and him and his brother Luke came to help. On another occasion, horse nails went in short supply and he came to my rescue when I was mega short on number six nails and he was on number seven. I had plenty of sevens and he had of sixes, so we just did a swap.

At big yards I often met up with Andrew and later Luke, who qualified as a farrier. We never interfered with each other's work unless we were asked. We chatted and joked with each other but that was as far as it went. Sometimes if one of us had finished and the others horse was playing up, we would probably help by holding the horse's head collar to make life easier.

Three or four years after starting his business, he was in the position to buy his own house and forge. His father, Matt, had sold the farm, and with a building at Andrew's, he started a farrier's supply business. He had a big variety of stock, and whatever any farrier wanted, we could rely on Matt to stock it. With him on my doorstep, anything I needed I didn't have to wait for it to be delivered. I could get same-day service and fetch what I wanted myself.

Brian Porter's big bang

Brian often called into the forge if he was passing. Sometimes he gave useful tips on how to go about jobs that were not so straightforward. On one occasion, he knew we had got to attend to three shire horses that wanted bevel shoes. Bevel shoes are where the ground surface of the shoe is wider than the hoof surface, thus giving the impression the horse has bigger feet. Making these shoes is not straightforward and more a two-man job. So when Brian called in, he got stuck in and would work with Paul while I worked with Willy.

While we were working, I noticed Brian had got a scrap bar of steel in the forge. He winked at me, and I had a good idea what he was up to. Paul thought the now burning piece of metal was to be part of the making of bevel shire shoes and kept saying it was burning away. Brian kept moving it around in the forge but didn't want it to stop burning. He was waiting for Paul to turn his back on him as he wanted to play a practical joke. When he saw his chance, as quick as a flash, he spit on the anvil and placed the burning bar in the spit, then hit the white-hot bar as hard he could with the hammer, causing a loud bang. Or more like an explosion.

Willy and I knew what was going to happen when Brian spit on the anvil and prepared ourselves with our hands over our ears. Paul with his back to us just about jumped out of his boots. When he returned back down to earth and recovered from being frightened to death, he wanted to know how Brian did it and wanted to have a go. Brian said, 'Well, Paul, get the bar of steel so it's really burning, and when the end looks like a giant sparkler, be quick and place it on the anvil and hit it as hard as you can.'

Brian never told him to spit on the anvil first, so when he got his steel to burning point, he placed it on the anvil and gave it one hell of a thud. Nothing happened, no bang or big noise Paul was expecting. So Brian said, 'You are not hitting it hard enough. Have another go.'

So Paul does the whole process again and still no bang.

This time Brian says, 'Let's wash the anvil down. It may be that it's not clean,' and splashes lots of water out of the water tub that was used for cooling off hot bars of steel.

The anvil was now nice and wet as Paul heats the bar up for a third time and was half-expecting nothing to happen again. This time, though, he hit it with such force the ear-bursting clatter was better than Brian's attempt. Unfortunately his attempt was so good he jumped out of his boots again, and although he didn't mean to, he flung the tongs and hot bar one direction and the hammer another. The noise he made took him by surprise. It had got nothing to do with how clean the anvil was but how wet it was.

WORKING IN THE WINTER ELEMENTS

One yard I went to where horses were on do-it-yourself livery, the setup was perfect for shoeing horses except for one problem: the lady who owned the stables, who I will call Gill. She had a barn-type building that housed about 20-odd stables. It was big enough if three farriers arrived at the same time, and if it was bad weather, there would have been room for us all to work under cover, including our vans. The problem was, Gill wouldn't allow us to work in the barn. She wanted us to work outside no matter what the weather. Of course if it was a nice sunny day, I would prefer to be outdoors. I didn't take kindly, though, when the wind chill was minus blooming Moscow and trying to snow when I was told I had to work outside.

I had already had a couple of run-ins with Gill when I went and shod one client's horse one afternoon a few months earlier. She told me in future I had to make appointments for the morning as she didn't want farriers disturbing the resting horses in the afternoon. Another time I got in trouble for finding a bucket of water to cool the horseshoes after I got them fitted. I had never before at other stables got in trouble for having to find a bucket of water but had more of an apology for having to help myself.

That morning when I was made to work in foul conditions outside, it was not on. Karen who owned the horse knew how I felt and tried her best to get me out of the elements, but Gill wouldn't allow it. I did shoe the horse and told Karen I didn't mind shoeing her horse but not at these stables ever again. I was relieved to hear the next time she wanted me she would be at another yard. I found other horse owners who were not my clients moved too as there were too many stupid rules.

Months later, I got a letter from Gill asking me if I could recommend her to some of my clients and what her rates would be. Also I would be welcome and could shoe horses at my convenience. It sounded to me that no one wanted to stable their horses with her.

CANCELLATIONS

From time to time, I had folk who had to cancel me for unforeseen circumstances. I didn't mind this as unforeseen circumstances crop up. Most of my clients would give me a day or so notice to give me the chance of rearranging my workload. One or two didn't.

One winter's morning I arrived on time for my 10 o'clock appointment and the lady who owned the horse was nowhere to be seen. The day in question was cold, but with no wind it was not uncomfortable to be out in the open air. Her old horse was stood at the field gate as if it was waiting for me. I pitied the poor thing as it was standing knee-deep in mud. I hoped when its owner arrived to unlock the padlocked gate, she would bring something to clean off the mud on the horse's legs. Then I realised she was not coming when I saw a note attached to an upturned bucket which had my shoeing fee in a plastic bag underneath. It read: *You will have to manage as it is too cold for me to hold my horse while you fit its shoes.'*

Well, I could have shod her horse but not in the muddy field. I would have shod it like I did all the others as the field was at the end of a cul-de-sac. There was a hardstanding outside the gate, and with it just a cold day, the weather was fine. I don't know how she thought I was going to manage on my own with the mud nearly up to her nag's kneecaps. It would have been impossible. Not only that, apart from climbing the gate with hot shoes several times and with no head collar to tie the horse up. I left a note and I wrote, *If it is too cold for you to get your horse out of the quagmire of a paddock, how do you expect me to work knee-deep in mud? Also I have a charge for wasting my time and will take a portion of the money you have left underneath the upturned water bucket for when I have shod your horse.*

On another occasion at other stables, I arrived to shoe two horses one morning. I was not too worried about how hard the rain was coming down as I could have got cover to work under. The horses' stables were not at the owner, I will call Pixie's, house but on the outskirts of the village. My heart sank when I saw the nags standing near a hedge two fields away from their stables. First, I thought she had got held up and would arrive shortly, but a quarter of an hour later I went to her house to be greeted by her husband. He never had an interest in the horses and told me his wife had gone to Leicester with her friend shopping. He told me she couldn't be bothered with it being such a foul day to catch her horses for me, and he certainly wasn't going to get involved.

I was fuming as I got to twiddle my thumbs for two hours. I knew I would be too early for my next call. As I was not near home, I had to spend two hours listening to the van radio.

A week later, Pixie rang to make another appointment and was not amused that I was charging her for wasting my time. I think at the time it was about £30 to shoe a horse but Pixie had to pay £80. She didn't like the £20 extra and said, 'Mick, that's robbery, it didn't cost you £20 in travel fuel.'

'I know it didn't, but it cost me £60 in lost earnings. If you had only let me know the night before, I could have arranged to go to another client,' I replied.

She reluctantly paid me the extra £20 in twenty pence pieces, trying to annoy me. Little did she know it did me a favour as I was always scratching for the right change for my son Nick's school bus fares and dinner money!

Another client, I will call Simon, would book me when his kid's pony's shoes were way overdue and desperate. He liked to think he was a whizz kid on computers in the days when most of us hadn't got a clue how to switch one on, never mind how to work one. He was always telling me how much money he was making before he had drunk his second cup of coffee at breakfast time. He gave me the impression that shoeing horses for a living was not as important to him as what he did. Mind you, what he told me I took with a pinch of salt as the family had to keep moving their pony to different locations for not paying the field rent. As for his cars, I think the local scrapyard would be their next owner. His wife though told a different story and talked as if they had money troubles when she once asked if I wouldn't mind waiting until the next time I shod the pony. That set off alarm bells ringing that Simon was not as rich as he was making out. If they can't pay for one set of shoes, how will they be able to afford two sets? I just told her my terms, and I wanted paying after each visit.

As for them cancelling me, I got used to Simon's voice the night before I was due having to cancel for one thing or another or if the weather was going to be cold. One occasion when I wouldn't have put it past him to arrange another date, he didn't. At the time there had been some hard frosts where the bushes and trees were white over. Although the temperature was near freezing, it was what I would call a nice cold, unlike when it is damp.

Even though I had not had a cancellation off Simon, I got bad vibes. The appointment was for one o'clock, and when I arrived at the field only to be greeted by the pony standing behind a big, locked gate, I expected the worst. I waited five minutes before my car phone rang. I had a good idea it would be Simon before I answered and knew he was going to tell me he wasn't on his way. He said it was too cold to stand in gateways and wanted to arrange another day. I was not a happy bunny and told him it was not fair to wait to cancel when I was at the field gate waiting for him. He had cancelled me too many times before, and I could have understood if he got some sort of emergency but not because it was a cold day. This time I thought it best that he ought to find another farrier. Animals still need attention and just because it's cold is no excuse to neglect them.

FOOT PROBLEMS

I shod horses for a vet called John and his wife. They used to compete at various dressage and show jumping competitions with their horses. Also they looked after horses that needed special veterinary care. I was asked on several occasions to shoe horses that needed remedial work for different lameness. One horse I was asked to attend was owned by a lady called Caroline Cotton, who I didn't know at the time. Her horse as far as I could see had nothing too much wrong apart from it being slightly flat-footed. I was told it didn't look sound, although it was not in too much discomfort. I took one look and thought if I had to shoe it, I would fit wide web shoes and seat them out. (Wide web is where the shoe covers more of the ground surface and seated is where the foot surface of the shoe is bevelled, so no pressure is on the sole of the foot.) How I shod this horse is how I would have done others which had the same problem regardless of whether a vet was involved. It would be like a human having a badly fitting pair of shoes. One would be able to walk but not with comfort.

A few days later after shoeing this horse, I bumped into John and he said the horse had gone back home, and Caroline thought I was God as her horse seemed to move much better. Two or three weeks later, I got another phone call off John asking me if I would go with him to Caroline's home to look at another of her horses that had got laminitis in both front feet. Also she wanted me to be her farrier. What he didn't tell me was it was one of the worst cases of laminitis we had ever seen. The pedal bones in both hooves were poking out through the soles of its feet.

The horse was in a bad way, and when we got Caroline to make us a coffee just to get her out of the way, I said to John, 'Does she know it may be bad news? We have known horses not half as bad being put to sleep.'

'I daren't tell her, Mick, we will have to give it a go and hope.'

The first thing we decided was for John to sedate the animal, and from past experience, we would chop out anything that looked infected. To some, it may look as if we are butchering the foot, and the only way I can explain it is to imagine you have a throbbing big blood blister under your fingernail. Once you have lanced it, the pain can go away. It is a bit the same with a horse. We are in fact lancing where the infection is, but in this case the pedal bones had rotated, which involved a bit more attention.

We decided to work on one foot on one visit and the other a couple of days later. We thought it would be too much for the horse to do both. Chopping out the infected bit and fitting what is known as heart bar shoes on both its feet in one go could cause the poor horse too much distress. (Heart bar shoes are shaped like a heart to give the hoof more support and help to push the pedal bones back into the right position, although there is bit more involved.) John and I recommended that heart bar shoes should be on for no more than four weeks as the hoof growth is accelerated with laminitis. We didn't want the toe of the foot getting too long. If that happens, the pedal bone will not go back to where it should be.

Caroline was a lady who did everything by the book, and it didn't seem fair she got these problems, unlike others who didn't give the same attention to their animals. Cutting a long story short, after a couple of months we saw a big improvement, although we had to overcome a few setbacks on the way. Then nine months later I fitted a normal set of shoes. Another six months later, she entered her first dressage competition. I still can't believe how bad this horse's laminitis was – I thought at best it would be pensioned off. Caroline got another eight years competing at shows with her horse before it passed away through old age. Needless to say, I looked after Caroline's horses until I retired.

I had a call to shoe a small pony and a horse from a couple who lived in a housing association house and not in a nice part of Leicester. I know most people that live in housing association houses are nice people, but for one or two sometimes the less said the better, and it applied to these two. Thank God that the horses were well away from where they lived. My van may have needed new wheels if I had to shoe at their house. Things often went missing.

The pony and horse seemed to look after themselves and lived in the filthiest conditions no other responsible horse owners would dream of. The stable on the edge of a field was knee-deep in muck and the horses' droppings.

Outside the paddock was one big slimy bog and a no-go area for shoeing horses. The only thing I could do was to shoe them on the pavement next to a main road and prayed the two nags behaved and stood still. I had a good idea that this may be another twopenny-ha'penny job. That's what I called those jobs where I only saw this sort of client once in a blue moon, and how right it turned out to be.

The husband had a permanent grin showing his yellow rotten teeth and was bragging how good he was. He told me he was a lorry driver and once got from Leicester to Ireland and back in a day, so straight away anything he said I took with a pinch of salt. I don't think even Lewis Hamilton would have done it that quickly in an articulated lorry. I think he had also forgotten how to look after his horses because it looked as if they were living on weeds or the sparse bits of grass left in the paddock.

The next time I saw the pony was 10 months later at the vet's. I did lots of work at this big veterinary practice at Chine House. I had a good working relationship with the eight equine vets. One vet I will call Simon asked if I would nip in to take shoes off a pony and trim its overgrown hooves. The poor thing was having difficulty standing, with its feet looking more like Ali Baba's. Simon told me the RSPCA were involved, and a member of the public had seen it laid flat out in the slimy, muddy field in the pouring rain and thought it was dead. It had to be lifted into a horsebox trailer to get it to the vets. The poor thing had just laid down because of its condition. I told Simon I knew the pony as I had shod it ages ago.

He had to sedate it for me, not that it was a difficult pony but just to help it stand for me while I trimmed its toenails. I said to Simon, 'It's got laminitis bad, I bet it's stress from its living conditions that's caused it and not having me for 10 months.'

Lots of people think laminitis is caused by horses getting too fat on lush grass but many other things stress-related can cause it, and this poor thing has had plenty of stress.

Trimming its feet, we didn't have much of a problem and I asked, 'What's going to happen to it, it's not going back to that muck hole is it?'

'They have promised the RSPCA that they will put a load of hardcore down, but... who knows? They both keep coming in to see it with the wife crying her eyes out, asking if it is going to die,' replied Simon.

'When are they due back? I hope you laid it on that it could die even though it hasn't got to that stage yet,' I grumbled.

'No, I haven't, she made me feel sorry for her instead of the pony, but you're right. I will lay it on a bit thick, Mick.'

We hadn't got the words out of our mouths when this couple appeared. Sure enough, the wife is hysterical saying, 'Will it die? We love it and can't live without it.'

I was in no more mood to pussyfoot with this couple and I don't think Simon was either, after all they did not think about the poor thing when it had to fend for itself, and we couldn't help ourselves telling them, 'Yes, the poor thing's chances are not good, yes it could die if it's not looked after better. You've got to clean its stable out and have its feet attended to regularly for it to stand a chance.'

Simon agreed with me that the woman now wailing was all a front. It looked like crocodile tears to me.

Their only concern was if the RSPCA was going to prosecute them.

We both said we will give them the chance to change their ways and we both would talk to the RSPCA on this occasion. That was going to be their chance to change their ways.

A year or so later, I was working in another yard when Simon arrived. I don't know what made me ask but had he seen or heard of that poor little pony. I certainly hadn't been called to trim its hooves.

'No, Mick, I haven't,' he replied.

He had just got the words out of his mouth when his mobile rang. By the look on his face and my name mentioned, I had the feeling it was something to do with those two characters.

His first words were, 'You are never going to believe it, it's that poor pony again. That was the RSPCA. They are on the way to the surgery with it. When can you come?'

I called in on the way home that same afternoon, but this time, the poor thing was beyond saving. The RSPCA, Simon and myself discussed its chances, and we all decided that the kindest thing was to put it to sleep. The RSPCA inspectors told me – which came as a surprise to me to learn – that the owners were blaming me for not turning up for appointments. Luckily the RSPCA knew me better than that and knew the real reason I had not turned up was that this couple had never booked me in the first place.

Next day I got a phone call off Mr Yellow Teeth, and he said the RSPCA might be calling me. He wanted me to lie and to tell them it was my fault as I had forgotten to book them in and that was why his pony's hooves were overgrown. He didn't know I was with the RSPCA and the vet when his poor pony had to be put down and I had already given a statement ready for his prosecution. No way would I lie to save his neck. I didn't view his animals as twopenny-ha'penny objects. I classed him and his wife as twopenny-ha'penny idiots.

PSORIASIS

It was autumn 1982, and Paul had gone off to broaden his skills elsewhere after working for me for six years, and now with Willy leaving as well, I had already decided I was not going to have any more apprentices and make the business smaller. I thought if I am off work with psoriasis and I have a young apprentice, he can't do anything by himself. How right it became, my psoriasis didn't peak, it got worse. My body was 75% covered in psoriasis.

Judy by chance saw a television program at the time about a treatment at the Dead Sea in Israel for psoriasis sufferers. Two weeks later, I was on my way to Israel for four weeks' treatment. The treatment was sunbathing and bathing in the Dead Sea. The Dead Sea's salt content and 24 different minerals including sulphur worked wonders on my skin in days. Mud from the Dead Sea was rubbed all over my body and after a period of time washed off in the Dead Sea. The sun's rays are filtered with it being the lowest elevation on earth, being 423 metres below sea level. The rays are filtered through a haze over the Dead Sea due to the water evaporating. The Jordan River flows into the Dead Sea and no water flows out, hence the haze forms and filters out lots of the sun's harmful rays. The air is very dry and oxygen-rich, higher with a 6% level than anywhere in the world.

In addition, the air is saturated with bromide and magnesium. This helps the nervous system calm down; you can't help zonking out and relaxing.

The Dead Sea is not at all refreshing to have a dip in. The water's high salt concentration level is 350 grams per litre. This is what gives the water the buoyancy. That is why we can float reading a book. It is not advisable to splash about in case saltwater gets in the eyes, and it also stings other sensitive regions on delicate parts of the body in the nether region. I never asked the ladies about their private sensitive bits, but a man's undercarriage is very sensitive to the Dead Sea, especially when suffering with psoriasis. I found that out on my first visit when I went in the water and half sat, half laid down. It is advisable for any male who has psoriasis near his undercarriage to practise doing handstands under the shower before visiting the Dead Sea. It took me less than five seconds to get out of the salty water and run to the shower to smooth my stinging nether region. The sting was terrible, and if I could have done a handstand under the shower, I would have done, if it would have helped my smarting crown jewels.

After forcing myself to go in the Dead Sea four or five times a day and mastering the technique of doing handstands under the shower (just joking), the stinging does go away. The same for sunbathing, you have to discipline yourself. My day started at seven in the morning with breakfast, eight o'clock down on the beach for the first dip in the sea. (After a week I could stay in the water longer, usually about 15 minutes.) Sunbathe until midday with more dips in the sea. Take a couple of hours out of the midday sun, have lunch, then back for more punishment at four until six pm. I did this same routine every day for four weeks, and God was it worth it. I had a new body without no horrible drugs.

Two years later, I had the chance to go back to the Dead Sea, but this time it was for a top-up. My skin was not too bad but this time it was only for a fortnight. Another fellow psoriasis sufferer who was at the Dead Sea when I was there two years before got in touch. He had started organising his own trips and offered me a cheaper visit. I could have used this trip as a holiday, but I still kept my strict routine and, with it being June, my tan looked as if I came from a Mediterranean country. On my return home, an Asian friend thought my suntan was overtaking his.

I had been to the Dead Sea four times, and each time I felt as if I came home with a new body. The third time in 1985, it was again more for a top-up, although psoriasis was breaking out more by the day. If I hadn't gone when I did, it might have become desperate in a week's time. At the time, Judy was pregnant with my youngest son Nick, and I didn't want the extra burden of having to worry over my skin when he was born. So that is why I booked another Dead Sea visit to make sure.

The fourth time in March 1987, I was desperate. The weather was bitterly cold, and with me losing so much skin, I couldn't keep warm. Putting greasy ointment on was horrible in freezing weather. The only place I could get comfortable was in a warm bath. The trouble was when I got out, my skin would go dry and scaly in seconds. It looked like butterfly wings stuck to me.

I was in nearly the same state as when I was in hospital 10 years before.

I had another Dead Sea trip booked and tried to carry on working until I went. To keep money coming in, I tried shoeing one horse in the morning and one in the afternoon. I say one in the morning because of the state I was in, it took me all morning to shoe one horse. Psoriasis, though, did beat me one bitterly cold morning when I went to shoe a client's horse. My body wouldn't bend without my skin cracking and bleeding. If I wanted to turn to look to the side or behind me, I had to turn my whole body. I was walking stiff-legged because my knees wouldn't bend. Psoriasis again covered 90% of my body.

That morning one of the horses I had booked in belonged to a lady I will call Rosemary, who was a very successful businesswoman, who took one look at me and said, 'Mick, you must be mad to work in that state, it looks painful. Why don't you just go straight home once you have shod my horse?'

I had to laugh and said to her, 'I haven't to go home before I have shod your horse then and forget everybody else's.'

I knew she didn't mean it the way she had said it, I did shoe her horse, and I did take her advice and go home afterwards, the others I cancelled. Psoriasis had won again until I had another session in Israel.

Psoriasis came and went over the next seven years, nothing too drastic to stop me from working. Then late in 1994 with the breakdown of my marriage, psoriasis started to get really angry again. This time I couldn't nip off to the Dead Sea because I had got Nick to look after. Nick was born in December 1985, 13 years after Karen.

I had got full custody of my eight-year-old son. Judy had now left, and I was living with my two sons, Nick and Chris. My daughter Karen had already moved out due to the friction between her and her mother. Chris and Karen, now in their twenties and a lot older than Nick, were a rock to me. No doubt they would have looked after him if I had gone to get more treatment at the Dead Sea, but I decided to go to the doctor.

The doctor got an appointment for me to see a skin specialist within days. The specialist told me about this PUVA (Psoralen and ultraviolet A radiation). This involved me taking four Psoralen tablets by mouth a couple of hours before I had my ultraviolet A radiation in a special unit at the hospital. The first two sessions, twice a week, lasted for 15 seconds.

The next sessions double, and after four to five weeks, 15 to 20 minutes had built up. These tablets also make the eyes sensitive to sunlight, so dark glasses need to be worn for 24 hours. It was a bind going to the hospital twice a week, but with the appointments being at eight o'clock in the morning, I did not lose much of my working day.

After five weeks of treatment, my skin was left with no trace of psoriasis. PUVA also left me with one hell of a suntan. I got asked quite often if I had been away on holiday to somewhere nice and hot. Unfortunately after five PUVA treatments over six years, I was advised not to have any more due to all the radiation my body had had.

The next two years I was under a skin specialist on three monthly appointments. I was prescribed Dovonex ointment which seemed to keep psoriasis at bay for a few weeks. My hopes were soon to be shattered again with daily eruptions multiplying faster than I could rub bucket loads of the stuff into my skin. It was as if psoriasis got immune to whatever ointment was used. That's what it feels like, any new ointment seems to work only for a short while. The psoriasis gets used to it, and no matter what is tried, it multiplies daily.

Ointments, the greasier the better, tend to make the skin comfortable for only a short period of time. On one occasion late one afternoon, I was nowhere near finished my day's work when my skin was getting really uncomfortable. John Craven, an old vet friend, arrived at the stables I was working at. He noticed I was uncomfortable and asked if a jar of his own brand of pink ointment would help. John's ointment was his own made recipe which was coloured pink for animals with skin infections.

I knew it was greasy and being desperate I rubbed a little on my wrists and arms. It was instant relief. Ten minutes later, I had gone into an empty stable and done my back and legs too. It had quite a strong aroma but I didn't care as it helped me to finish my day's work.

At the next stables, the horse owner kept sniffing when I was close to them. I would ask, 'Can you smell John Craven's pink ointment?'

'Oh, that's what is. What have you been up to, Mick, to stink like that?'

'I had become uncomfortable with psoriasis; my skin was so dry and sore, and he produced a jar of his pink ointment as I'd not got my own ointment with me.'

'That's for animals. Is it safe for humans to use?' they asked.

I didn't know what ingredients went into John's pink ointment, nor did anybody else. He took this secret remedy to his grave when he died years later. Lots of animal owners swore by it as it got results, not just with horses but other animals too. Pink ointment didn't cure psoriasis, though, but it certainly helped to take the soreness away whenever I was desperate.

In October 1988, psoriasis was threatening to erupt again. Not as bad as previously but bad enough. I had mentioned it to our Cypriot friend Andros, who owned the local fish and chip shop, how I thought another trip to the Dead Sea was looming. He said he and his cousin George were going to Cyprus on business, what was stopping me going with them? He knew the sun was good for my complaint, and with it still in the high twenties temperature-wise, it might help me.

My first thought was I can't as I had too much work booked in. OK, if it was like the last outbreak, yes, I wouldn't have thought about work. This time it was just threatening. Judy thought I should go, and what about asking Paul to do my work while I was away. Although Paul had left me six years before, we still kept in touch when he was back in the UK. He lived with his parents in Sileby, the same village as me. I say he was back because in those days Paul did a lot of travelling back and forth to America and Australia, still shoeing horses.

I got hold of Paul and asked if he got anything planned for the next fortnight, and if not, would he do my work.

So three days later I was sitting on an aircraft on the way to Cyprus. Paul was only too pleased to help me out as he was at a loose end for a month. He used my van, tools and forge as his were still in America. After all, he knew most of my clients as he shod horses for them when he worked for me.

One thing, though, that didn't help my stress levels was Andros's cousin George's driving. They had hired a brand spanking new car with only five hundred or so miles on the clock. George liked to drive at breakneck speed and left braking until the last moment. The last moment for braking was too late one night when we were on the way to have dinner with an old friend of Andros's called Yannis. George was driving again with his foot flat to the floor and shouting obscenities at other drivers that they were not getting out of his way quick enough; he never gave it a thought it was him who was the lunatic. George approached a bend far too fast, and when he hit the brake pedal, we were already embedded in the side of a very irate lady's car. After Andros and I managed to calm George and the lady down and exchanged the necessary details, both cars were still driveable – just. Although our car had the wing caved in on the front wheel, we managed to prise it away, and with only the nearside headlight working, we managed to arrive at Yannis's, thankfully with Andros driving. He was the opposite of George.

A day or so later, Andros and George arranged to meet me after they had finished what business they had to attend to. I arranged to meet them at a café called Michaels. When they arrived, I couldn't help noticing the passenger back door of the car wasn't shut properly and had looked bent. Also when I got in, I had to get in through the front door and climb over the seat because a rope was tied from one back door to the other. That was because the bent door would have been flapping about if it was not tied to the other one. I found it was George who had caused the damage. They had given a lift to someone and when the person got out, George never gave them the chance to shut the door and reversed with it still open into a lamp post, thus bending it.

I was glad I wasn't going to be with them when they returned this wreck of a car to the hire company. I was on an earlier flight than them. Even though my stress levels rose with George's driving, the warm sunny climate did help my skin complaint and I thought I wouldn't mind living in Cyprus one day.

Paul had no trouble doing my round and often came and gave me a hand on a busy day.

Years later, Paul got a contract in France. He was asked if he could shoe horses that pulled Gypsy-type caravans that folk hired for their holidays. He had seen the horses he got to shoe when he was on holiday and some had shire-size feet. When his holiday finished, he came to see if he could use my forge to make these large horseshoes. He had arranged to go back and shoe them. What bothered him, though, was he'd not got anywhere he could use as a forge in France. He was also hoping if one client saw his work it could attract others.

One morning I left on my rounds to the sound of the forge roaring and Paul making a dozen sets of these shire-size horseshoes on a blazing hot day. I thought good luck as these heavy shoes are not as easy as the bog-standard smaller type. With my forge next to a pub, I was told by the landlord that Paul came in at lunchtime.

He ordered a pint of shandy, and before the landlord had time to give him his change, he wanted another as the first one didn't touch the sides. He finally got his shoes made, and his plan worked with him setting his farriery business up in France and still shoeing horses there 30 years later.

MARY'S HORSES

It would be late 80s, early 90s, I was asked to shoe for a lady I will call Mary. I was told to watch her by many folk, but none would say why. I took this to be sour grapes that she had asked to be on my books, but their facial expression didn't seem to mean she was bad at paying her bills. I thought if she was one for not paying her bills, I would have heard about her as us farriers did stick together and warn others about anyone who was a bit dodgy, but she paid me well.

Mary had five horses of her own plus about another five that were in livery at her stables. I ended up with the whole yard to shoe. At the time I may have been a little naïve but Mary always looked immaculate. At other stable yards, the girl grooms never wore makeup when at work, even though they were attractive, but Mary always looked ready as if she was going for good night out. Her makeup matched whatever designer outfit she wore. Her hair always looked groomed as if she just left the hairdressers. She drove a top-of-the-range sports car, plus owned a nice property with a dozen stables and several paddocks. Also she employed a young girl to help with the running of the stables. I wondered how a young woman could manage to afford all this as she must only be in her late twenties. Perhaps she was from a wealthy family who bought her the place. I didn't know, but to me she was the perfect client. Always paid me well on every visit. It was not for me to say how she should dress for mucking out the horses' stables, but I did wonder how she could afford her lifestyle.

About six months later, I found out by accident where her wealth came from. It was a Wednesday afternoon when her girl groom had her half day. Mary had me booked to shoe her five horses, so it meant I was there for the whole afternoon. Her nags were well behaved and stood patiently while I fitted them with new shoes. I was asked if I would be OK on my own as she needed to nip off for an hour or so, as she had to meet a client. I never thought anything of it as I would be fine by myself. Five minutes or so after she left, the phone rang in her tack room. I ran to answer, and before I said a word, a man's voice asked could he book an appointment.

I replied, 'What's your number? I'll get her to ring you back when she's free.'

He then asked was I there doing business.

Not thinking, I said, 'Yes.'

'Oh, I am sorry to have disturbed you,' he said and hung up.

Ten minutes later it rang again, another guy saying he would meet her Saturday night at the Mayfair in London. His room was... By the time she came back, I had started to twig what her profession was from the tone of the many calls I answered and had a list of customers who wanted an appointment. Not only that, I felt like a pimp taking bookings for her. Yes, she wasn't the type plying her services on the streets but hotels where any ordinary folk would have to take out a second mortgage to afford to stay the night. She only worked from Thursday evening to Sunday night and travelled back home from London on the Monday morning. I thought that my fees had come from immoral earnings. Well if it did, it paid well.

ONE DAMP DAY

It was a cold, damp winter's day when I suppose my clothes never smelled their best. It was a day when it never actually poured with rain but was more of a light drizzle. I felt the weather was not bad enough to stop me working outdoors. I had an appointment at one large stables, and I was there for several hours. Although I could have got in a stable, it was hard work through them being on the dark side and cramped. So with a nice clean concrete yard outside, I could get on better. I thought with it only light drizzle I would not get too wet.

After six hours, I was soaked. My chunky woollen pullover was not just wet but had collected all the burning of hoof odours. The trouble is, and I think I can speak for other farriers, we can often stink. We don't realise we do as I suppose we just get used to it.

Anyway after getting soaked, I called at a B&Q store as I was doing a bit of DIY at home and needed paint and other materials. I was up and down the aisles looking for what I wanted when I noticed staff running from aisle to aisle, shouting.

'It's over here, too. No, come here, I think it is amongst the shelves, hey up it's down this aisle now, can't see anything but it's all over the place. God, we've got to do something, it could be a big bugger, right down here now. Where the hell has it come from?'

I thought it must be a rat or mouse they had seen, and now other staff and other customers including myself were now searching under the display cabinets to see if we could spot the pesky little rodent. Staff were by now getting really concerned, and one then another would be shouting something like this:

'Let's get the authorities in?' I hear one shout. 'Yes, we will have to. Do we evacuate the building, or should I ask the manager to r—.' 'Bugger it, I'll ring,' shouts another. 'It's down this aisle and over here,' shouts another. 'Let's not panic; it may be nothing much,' bellows a young lad. 'We ought not to… Let's not wait for something dreadful to happen,' says another assistant.

When I heard one staff member say should they evacuate the building, I quickly got my goods and went to pay before the building got evacuated. Surely, they were not going to get everyone to leave for a mouse. Then a member of staff announced over the loudspeaker system.

'Please do not panic, but everybody leave the building. It may not be serious, just a precaution, thank you.'

I had just paid for my goods when this announcement was made and asked the assistant on the checkout what was the problem just as a big red fire engine appeared outside.

'Strong smell of burning. Didn't you smell it?' she replied.

'Burning smell. Oh no, I thought it was a mouse or something, I even looked under the cabinets and shelves to see if I could see the culprit. Now it is me who is the culprit.'

'Why is it you?' she replied.

'Smell my jumper. I'm a farrier, and with it being a damp day, the smoke from the burning hooves are stuck to my damp chunky pullover, and I have a feeling it's me who is leaving a burning trail up and down the aisles of the store, sorry,' I said sheepishly.

When the fire engine turned up, I felt an arrow pointing above my head and staff shouting, it's him, it's him. Needless to say, my face was as red as the fire engine.

Other times I have often left shops thinking their shop was on fire. There again, most farriers have stories of causing alarm in shops or offices from the smell of burning on their clothing.

Another time Phyl's car was in the garage for a small repair so I would drop her off at work in the mornings and pick her up in the evening. She worked as an accountant for an air freight company at East Midlands Airport. I didn't have any set time to pick her up in the evenings as she always had plenty to do, and she often worked late anyway. Phyl had often moaned that her office could be a bit on the chilly side, but to me the whole building felt like a sauna. Again it was on a cold, damp day when I went to pick her up straight from work.

All the staff in her office had left for home apart from her managing director and the financial director when I got there. It was probably around six thirty. The three of them were in Phyl's office looking at accounts.

When I walked in, I was greeted as if I was part of their work family. I knew most of the staff from functions such as dinners that many air freight companies were involved with. This time, though, was the first these guys had met me dressed in my work clothes. Other times I would be all scrubbed up and dressed in a smart evening suit, but this occasion I kept hearing them say to Phyl, 'Really you might as well go – *sniff* – Don't want to hold Mick up – *sniff* – we can – *sniff* – finish it – *sniff* – off tomorrow.'

At the time I didn't think anything of it and said, 'Oh, don't worry about me. You finish what you are doing.'

I met them all at firm's functions but not dressed in jeans and pullovers impregnated with odours of wet horse and burnt hoof, even though they knew what I did for a living. I think when I left with Phyl, they may have opened one or two windows even though the temperature outside was near freezing.

On the way home, she asked me if it was possible to pick her up at three thirty next day.

A likeable rogue

When we first moved to Sileby and I worked non-stop getting my forge up and running, I decided, one night, a pint of beer was in order. On entering a local pub near our home and not knowing a soul, I became aware lots of eyes were staring at me. After a few minutes, one of the locals came to have a chat. He spoke in a rough and ready voice sprinkled with one or two words that again brought more of an essence to the sentence. He was in his late 20s, single, had no teeth, was smoking rollups, and dressed in clothes that looked to have gone out of fashion in the 1940s. His thick, black, long hair was down to his shoulders and he had a moustache that looked to be in two halves due to him having a hair lip. The long overcoat he wore also looked as if it had seen better days. His woolly hat had paint and god knows what embedded in it, and his work boots had never seen any polish from new. First, I thought these were his work clothes but I soon realised they were his going out gear too. He reminded me of a cross between Benny from *Crossroads* and Claude Greengrass from *Heartbeat*. Also he walked with a slight limp. His name was Dave Belcher, and on my first meeting, the impression I got of him was not good.

I asked how he had hurt his leg, expecting it to be no more than a bit of a simple knock or stiffness. It turned out he had a false one. He had lost his leg in a motorbike accident a few years earlier. It was not his fault, and he had got awarded compensation which bought him his house. He soon pointed out that it did not stop him from climbing ladders or doing jobs many able-bodied folk wouldn't think of attempting.

I also found out Dave had a talent which I didn't have. He could go out on a night, no, every night, with no money and manage to have a few drinks at other fellow drinker's expense. I know I copped for a couple that first night and noticed often he had two pints on the go at the same time which others had got in for him.

That night he asked had we got settled in and what did I do for a living. If I needed any help to give him a shout. He told me he liked to do painting and decorating but could turn his hand to most things. Little did I know that after that first meeting, we would become lifelong friends! He was true to his word. Yes, he could turn his hand to most things, but one thing I soon found out, you didn't pay him until he'd finished. He couldn't help himself, once he had money it would be gone on fags and beer. Then he would promise he would finish whatever job he was doing tomorrow, which never came.

I can remember one night we needed a babysitter for my youngest son Nick who was about five at the time. We had three children. Nick was born 13 years after Karen our second child. I can't remember what or where we were going, and with the usual babysitter cancelling at late notice, it was Dave who offered to look after him. He had always had a soft spot for Nick. Loads of times he would either be playing or building something or other with him. I had a scrap woodpile that had to be chopped up for our wood burner oven. (Similar to an Aga). Dave decided to recycle the best bits to build a slide for Nick. Then on another day he built him a child's wheelbarrow. When Nick got two rabbits, Dave built him a hutch. Nothing ever was too much trouble.

One morning while making my horseshoes, Dave poked his head through my forge door and commented on how the rendering was falling off the bottom half of my forge's outside wall. The top bit looked OK, and did I want him to have a go at renewing the bad bits. Later that day when I returned home from work, I found my workshop with no rendering from the ground to four feet up. He stripped the lot off and then told me he had never done rendering before and that it was going to be a bit of trial and error. *Oh no*, I thought, *what have I let myself in for here*?

Next morning, I had left on my rounds before Dave had surfaced and wondered what was going to happen to my forge's wall. Well what a shock I got later that day. A beautiful professional job. First, I thought it was somebody he knew had finished it, but Judy assured me it was his own work.

'Hope it stops on,' he told me when I saw him later that evening.

He used a mixture of some old sand, cement, concrete, and pebbles left over from two or three years before when we altered the forge. I had often thought it may be past its sell-by date as the contents felt rather solid. He just kept jabbing the old solid bags of cement with a shovel to loosen it up. Then mixed the cement with a bag of concrete and some pebbles and plastered it on the wall. As for the pattern in the rendering, while still wet he had jabbed it with the yard brush bristles to good effect.

Twenty-odd years later when we were thinking of putting the place up for sale, the rendering at the top half had started to fall off. Professional builders were called and they said it would be best to take the lot off and start again. Seeing as we were selling, we thought it best for it to look nice and agreed a price.

A week or so later, a guy from the builders arrived to start stripping the old rendering off ready for his mate to come the next day to apply new mortar. I went off to do my day's work and I returned later that afternoon to find only the top half stripped off.

'Is there some sort of mistake? I thought we agreed to do the whole lot?' I asked.

'We did but there's a problem. We can't shift the bottom bit. Somehow, we will have to try to match it up,' was his reply.

I then told him the story how my mate did the bottom half and it was a bit of trial and error. This guy didn't think there was any error, considering Dave's job was now more than 20 years old. One of the best bits of rendering he had ever seen.

Another morning, Dave arrived on crutches minus his false leg just before I left to do my day's work. With the weather hot and sweaty, it made his stump sore. He'd come for one of the many rides out with me. My first call of the day meant opening two big heavy gates into Colin and Glynis Foster's yard. This meant lifting and tugging, and with Dave in no fit state to manage them, I would have to do them myself.

When I had driven the van into the Foster's yard and closed the gates, Colin came out of his house and asked, 'What's up with him, couldn't he have opened the gates for you, Mick?'

'Oh, he's legless,' I replied.

'What, at nine o'clock in the morning?' mutters Colin.

Then Dave emerges from the van, and Colin now has a face full of horror.

'Oh, sorry, mate, when Mick said you were legless, I took it you were pissed,' says Colin.

We all saw the funny side, and although Colin had met Dave several times before, he had never twigged he had an artificial leg. Also John Craven my vet friend called in and he had never realised he had lost his leg. When Dave said he wasn't wearing his false leg because the warm weather was making his stump sweaty and sore, and the lotions he got from the doctors had little effect, John said, 'Try some of my pink ointment,' which Dave found worked the best.

While at the Foster's, Glynis had an issue with string hay nets which she used for feeding her horses. They were expensive and didn't last long, she moaned. Dave suggested she could surely make her own with all the nylon string the hay and straw bales were tied up with. She had tried that but couldn't get them right.

'It's harder than you think,' mutters Glynis.

'Well, while Mick's shoeing t'hosses, I'll have a go,' replied Dave.

Here's a guy with no knowledge of anything to do with horses having a go at making hay nets for them. Two hours later, he had sussed it out and made the most perfect hay net.

Now he had mastered the technique and had got quicker at making them, he was collecting nylon bale string from every stable we went to. He could see a nice little earner. After all, the string was only going to get thrown away and most stables were all keen to get rid of it. He sold hundreds, then sales started to slow up. The trouble was they were far more superior to the others and never seemed to wear out. They were lasting for years not months, unlike the expensive ones.

As I have mentioned, Dave's language could be somewhat colourful. I know one or two of my clients spoke in the same dialogue as him but most were quite refined. I can remember one day a titled lady wanted a chat to me about her old horse. It had its fair share of lameness with one thing or another and with age against it, its prognosis was not good. It had always been her pride and joy and faithful to her. Anything that could keep it going in some sort of comfort she wanted to try. I was just the same with my dogs; I didn't want to hear that their life was coming to an end. Anyway we must have talked for 10 to 15 minutes of what to do next when from the front of my van we heard Dave's voice with a roll-up stuck in his mouth shout, 'Hey up, missus, isn't it about time you were getting kettle on for a mug of tea, the bloody thing's ready for knacker's yard.'

I think she saw my face change colour, but also, I think she saw I needed to dig a hole quick, to bury Dave.

We didn't get our cup of tea. Luckily, she did want me to shoe her horse but not to take that dreadful man with me there ever again. I did have a word with him when we were going down the road that you couldn't talk to my refined clients like he did. I know that I could have agreed with him sometimes, but it was not our place to tell her horse was knackered.

To which he replied, 'They all come into world like us, and they are off out the same.'

'I know, Dave, but while they are here, I want to make money out of them,' I answered.

My friend also liked to show off, especially with the ladies. He was far from being a handsome looking guy, and his choice of attire would also have put off most women; it never stopped him flirting with a women's darts team. He'd gone for a pint and bought a bag of crisps and was trying to devour his snack with no teeth – one would have thought he was in a gurning competition. While chewing on a crisp, he took one of the lady's darts and jabbed it in his leg and never flinched, and just pulled ugly faces trying to munch his crisps with his bare gums. All the women looked in amazement at a guy sticking a dart in him with no sign of pain.

'Didn't it hurt?' one asks.

'Mind over matter,' replies Dave, still trying to chew a crisp.

'Do it again,' another demands.

So Dave sticks another dart in his leg and carries on eating his snack.

'How do you do that? You sure it doesn't hurt? Can I have a go?' asked another one.

'Sure, tell yourself it won't hurt and do it,' he answers.

So she told herself it won't hurt and stuck a dart straight into Dave's good leg. None of them realised he had a false leg. They all thought it was some trick, and with one of the women wanting a go, Dave thought she was going to use her own leg.

My dogs

Over the years I have had several dogs, and all but one accompanied me on my farrier rounds. First, Tinker, a Jack Russell who came into my life not long after Judy and I got married in 1970. He loved to come with me, especially to a little riding school run by a Mr Clark and his wife. Their own children were grown up and left home, but the Clarks seemed to like to look after everybody else's. All the kids loved the hustle and bustle of the riding school, mucking out stables, fetching ponies and horses in ready to be groomed and tacked up ready for a client's riding lesson. The Clark's stables were different to the others. He was a kind man who never seemed to be rushed or flustered and had his school running like clockwork. I never once heard him get cross and shout and order his many young helpers about like other places. He politely asked them if they could go do whatever and never got a moan back. I had often commented his place resembled a kindergarten more than a riding school but like he said, he would sooner have the kids with a hobby than hanging out on some street corner.

My little Jack Russel, Tinker, loved to come to the Clark's stables too and became a big favourite with the children. They found out that if they started to sing, he loved to join in, howling at the top of his voice, not exactly in tune with the children but he enjoyed himself. His other skill was football. Often, I would be engrossed in my work and think, *Oh God, where is Tinker?* It was usually on the riding club's lunch break, and Mr Clark would say, 'Oh, don't worry, he's playing football in the back paddock.'

There he would be, running and dribbling the ball with his nose, never trying to bite or burst it. The kids even fought about whose team he was going to be in. He was their star player. Riders would start arriving for riding lessons and would start watching a dog equivalent to a Stanley Mathews. They would be shouting and clapping like football supporters, watching the skills of my Jack Russell. Mr Clark said he was going to give up teaching people to ride horses when it was farrier day and charge people to watch football instead. Tinker just loved kids; he would play and keep them amused all day.

Even at home with my own children, he was very protective of them, especially my daughter Karen. Before they were born, friends and relations were saying we must watch him with a newborn baby. Don't let him feel he's left out and having to take a back seat to the baby. So we made sure we made a fuss of him too when Chris arrived. What happened? Nothing. Tinker didn't mind Chris, he never bothered him when he was a baby, played with him when he was a toddler. He just accepted him as part of the family.

It was a different story when Karen was born. He got it into his head that he must protect her at all costs. My grandparents were staying with us, helping to look after Chris while Judy was in hospital giving birth. In those days, a woman stayed in hospital a lot longer after childbirth than they do nowadays. My grandfather never got to visit Judy and Karen in hospital, so never saw his great-granddaughter until she arrived home. Karen was in a carrycot on the settee, and I said to my grandfather to go and see her. Tinker had other ideas. He was already sitting on the floor next to the settee and started to growl in an aggressive manner at my grandfather.

You are not going near her, I am guarding her, came his warning, and that is how he was with Karen for the rest of his life. Always near her, especially if she was ill. You would find him laid next to her, trying to give her comfort and support.

His little life probably ended sooner than later, aged 12. He got attacked by a dog running off its lead while we were on holiday in the summer of 1981 at Seaton in Devon. We were told by some of the locals that it was vicious, and the attack on him was not its first. The woman who owned it begged us not to get the police involved and would pay the vet's fees. Poor old Tinker had his flesh ripped open to reveal big gaping wounds that required several stitches and a two-day stay at the vets. He did survive the attack but started to have little seizures afterwards, until a big one ended his life a year later.

Not long after Tinker had died, Kim and Zoe came into our life, both bitches and mongrels from a stray dog kennels. Kim was more a stay-at-home dog, who liked her walks and meeting the children out of school. Zoe was the more adventurous type. She loved to come to work with me every day. Outside our house and garden, she was quite a gentle dog. Anyone could stroke her and she made so many friends amongst my horsey clients. At home, she could be aggressive, especially with any men who dared to walk through the garden gate at the side of our house which led into the back garden. Women and children were no problem, she would let them in. Men, if she didn't know them, no way was she going to let them in.

Zoe used to love the days when my old mate, Dave Belcher, came for his usual day out with me on my farriery round. I will always remember the days at a stable in the middle of the countryside. No houses or neighbours in sight, just hilly fields and loads of rabbit warrens.

Dave would say, 'Come on, Zoe, let's have a look for some rabbits,' and off the two would go.

I had two horses to shoe at this particular call, and I would see the pair of them together investigating the many rabbit holes for an hour and a half or so. Not they ever caught any. If they did, I doubt either of them had a killer instinct in them.

The funny thing about Kim and Zoe was that Kim picked me at the dog kennels. She was one of about six dogs let out of the compound. All the other dogs ran around the kennel's yard and were not at all interested that we could offer them a new home. Kim had other ideas. As soon as she was out of the door, she launched herself at me and gave me a good licking.

It was her way of saying, *I love you, please pick me, I'm a good dog, I won't give you any bother, please, please, please.*

So that is how Kim and I met.

Zoe on the other hand was still in her little kennel and looked the most timid, unloved dog on the planet.

She didn't move, and Judy took a shine to her. We had to drag her out of the kennel, and the dog sanctuary people warned us she might not be the easiest dog to get attached to. How wrong they could be. Not only was she faithful to all the family and Kim too, but she became my workmate for the next five years of her short life. It was ironic that Judy picked her and I picked Kim, but she ended up being Judy's dog and Zoe mine. Anywhere I went, Zoe was with me. She didn't mind sitting in the van at the odd call where dogs were not allowed out. It was something she seemed to understand and never made a fuss. The van windows could be wide open and she never offered to escape.

These two dogs were not only good with children but babies too. Nick my youngest son was sitting propped up on the settee while Judy nipped into the kitchen. She had only been left seconds but Nick had started to slip over. Not off the settee but onto his side, and before he did, Judy found both dogs sitting either side of him propping him up. How did they know?

Zoe's short life came to a tragic end when we didn't realise she had tried to chase after our car. We were having building work done on our house, and with the builders in and out of the garden, the gate had got left open. We had to go out and assumed both dogs were shut in the house, but somehow, we must have locked Zoe out. She must have seen us leave and not wanting to miss out on a car ride, she tried to run after us and then got hit by another car. On returning back home and realising Zoe was not in the house, we started to panic. On searching the village to no avail and hoping on hope that she may turn up somewhere or just come home, we all had a feeling that something dreadful had happened. An hour and a half later, our suspicions became true when John Craven the local vet rang. The car driver who hit her took her to him, still alive but with terrible injuries, and John had no chance to save her and had to put her to sleep.

Next day at work without Zoe was strange, I had lost my workmate. Zoe had gone everywhere with me. She loved the hustle and bustle of the day-to-day life at the many stables. It was not only the family and me who missed her, it was my clients too. Yes, Zoe was a very different dog from the first time we saw this unloved timid thing at the dog sanctuary five years previously. She was really enjoying the farrier life and I was pleased that I was a part of it. I hope Zoe thought the same of me.

Two or three months after Zoe's death, Holly a seven-year-old collie cross came into our lives. She too was a rescue dog and fitted in with our family life from day one. Kim accepted her, and there was never a fallout between the two. They too became best of friends, only Holly, too, was not a stay-at-home dog. She was just the same as Zoe and loved going to work with me. Lots of my clients fell in love with her friendly nature. It amazed me how Zoe, Kim and Holly needed no training. I could have walked through the middle of a town with no lead and none of the dogs would have left my side. Mind you, I only did this once when I realised I didn't have Holly's lead, but I am sure I could have trusted the others as well.

I talked to my dogs as friends and I was sure they understood every word I said to them. I am sure they learned to understand the tone of my voice. I never got cross with them.

Holly became my new workmate for the next seven years. She seemed to take over from Zoe, and she in no time got to know all the ins and outs of my farrier round. At one call, I usually had to knock on the horse owner's door to let them know I had arrived as the stable was round the corner from their house. Holly soon twigged, and as soon as we got out of the van, she would go and knock on the door, OK a bark, while I unloaded my tools.

Another time, Judy needed to go and stay with her mother in Ipswich for a few days when her mother fell and broke her shoulder. Both dogs were in the kitchen of our house when Judy commented, would I manage? Nick was going with her but what about the dogs? I said Holly would come to work with me and couldn't Kim go with her? She didn't mind a car ride to Ipswich. Straight away, Kim stuck her head up as if to say, *What, me going to Ipswich? I'm on for that.*

If I had said, can't you take Kim shopping with you to Leicester, she wouldn't have responded? She would sooner stop at home but going on holiday that's another kettle of fish.

One day while shoeing horses at stables that were near a field with sheep, Holly had never looked or tried to go into the field and chase them. That was until they escaped out onto the road. The farmer and one of his workers were trying to round them up when Holly decided she wanted to help. I was shouting for her to come back when I realised what she was doing. Farmers are known to shoot dogs if they are chasing their sheep but this farmer said to leave her, she was brilliant. What a natural sheepdog; she had had no training that I knew about, and how she worked the sheep must have saved the farmers no end of time. He also asked, did I want to sell her? A sheepdog like her is worth thousands, and where did I get her from? When I said from the stray dog sanctuary, he couldn't believe it. It didn't matter to me if she was good at rounding up sheep or not, she was always going to be my workmate.

Both Kim and Holly both showed their gentle nature when Nick my youngest son got two rabbits. Dave Belcher had built a super-duper rabbit hutch for them, but with the garden having a brick wall around it, the rabbits often just roamed free. They were never shut in their home, which had two apartments one side where they made a nest for a bed and the other for food and water. The main door was always left open for them to go out and in at their own free will.

Neither dog offered any sort of aggression to them. In fact Kim could be laid out on the lawn with the rabbits cuddled up with her. It was a joy to see them all getting along as friends and much nicer for the rabbits, too, instead of having to be locked up like prisoners all day.

Kim often amused us if someone was taking a photo. She made sure that she got in the picture too. I remember on one occasion when a relative wanted a photo of us. Judy, me and the kids got positioned perched on the settee, and just when the camera clicked, a dog's head appeared from behind Nick with what looked a doggy smile on her face.

She was a dog that never had anything go wrong with her health until the age of 12. The dog's water bowl was having to be filled up five or six times a day. We knew it couldn't be Holly as she was out with me all day. Judy started to watch Kim and noticed that as soon as she filled the dog's water bowl with fresh water, Kim would half empty it. Our vet John Craven confirmed our suspicions. Diabetes. So now we had to give injections of insulin every day for the rest of her life. That dog never once moaned about her condition and for the next nine months, things looked back to normal apart from her daily treatment. Every day she wanted to walk with Judy when she took Nick to school and, in the afternoon, to pick him up. Never a murmur on this mile and a half round trip. Then one day out of the blue she had difficulty on the homeward journey. Luckily it was more or less in spitting distance of our house, as her legs started to buckle beneath her. Judy thought she may need to get help to carry her home but slowly she did manage to struggle back. John was called and gave her an injection but I can't quite remember what it was and, although we didn't take her on any more long walks, she started to pick up again. Then a month later, she was back down again. With the downs starting to be more regular and lying down on her stomach to eat, we knew the end was near. This was confirmed one morning when we got up to see Kim still in her wet and pooed bed. The poor thing had not had the energy the night before to relieve herself in the garden. The twinkle had disappeared out of her big brown eyes, and the vet was called to put this wonderful dog to rest in peace.

Losing the other two was bad enough. I didn't have to have them put to sleep but with Kim, watching her being injected for the last time was heartbreaking.

Two years later, I lost Holly. Not that she had passed away but due to our marriage coming to an end. Judy had a few problems I won't go into and she wanted a divorce. She had come and gone before, and something me and the two eldest children never saw coming was when she asked me to leave Holly at home instead of me taking her to work. We just thought she needed Holly's company due to the many things happening in her head. At the end of that day, my eldest, Chris, got home before me and first thought we had a burglar visit. It appeared any item on its last legs, they had very kindly left for us. Then he twigged, his mother was nowhere to be seen. She had emptied the house and took my workmate. I must say, I really missed that dog.

ALLY

Oh, what can I say about Ally? Well, many things. I first met Ally at our village veterinary practice one Saturday morning in February 1995. It was a big concern that employed many vets, with eight who specialised mainly on the equine side. One vet had asked me to attend to a horse that needed a surgical shoe fitted due to a lameness problem. While there, one of the nurses, Bridget, told me I needed another dog and they had one that needed a good home. She was right. My head at the time was full of problems due to my marriage breakup, which was getting rather nasty. Also I had not had a dog since losing Holly 18 months previously. This lovely lady knew how much I enjoyed a dog's company and thought it might help to get my life into some sort of order. Ally was a three-year-old Labrador bitch, who'd had a rough start to life. The family who owned her before me kept her shut in a small shed all day and then moaned about her barking for hours on end. From what I was told, she had very rarely been taken out for a walk, and who could blame her from barking then running off as soon as the shed door was opened. The odd times that she escaped her prison, she was left to wander around the streets until a member of the public handed her in at the vets. Bridget knew Ally's ex-owners and had returned her loads of times. Then they told her the dog was a pain in the neck and they didn't want her back. When she told me that the animal rescue people were collecting her that afternoon, it made me make my mind up quickly. After finishing shoeing the horse, I ended up leaving with a dog sitting in the passenger seat of my van.

A week later, I had started to agree with Ally's last owners. Yes, she could be a pain in the neck. I had for years been used to arriving at stables and never having to worry about my other dogs. They all behaved themselves, but with Ally I often had to tie her on a long lead to save me time searching the countryside for her. Sometimes finding she still escaped by chewing through the rope that tethered her. I persevered, and six months later and with her behaviour improved, I found another side to her. With loads on my mind dealing with solicitors through a messy divorce, I found who my friends were. The best one was Ally. I could be sitting on my own in an armchair, wondering what the hell was going to happen next. My two sons who lived with me were not any trouble. They, too, gave me lots of support, but a dog I had known for just a short while would come up to me, put her front paws on my lap and press her face next to mine, then give me a lick as if to say, *Well, I love you.*

About the same time, I had a holiday booked with my two sons and left her with a friend, Liz Hancox, who had a small stables in the village. I had to get my parents to look after our house while we were away due to my ex breaking in several times and helping herself to items that I had replaced after she helped herself to most things previously. I thought them having to look after a dog that, still at times, had a mind of her own could be too much. That's why Liz offered since Ally knew her dogs and had big paddocks to play in all day.

Liz soon found that a big five-bar gate was no obstacle for a fit Labrador. A farmer visiting Liz saw my dog one morning walk up to the gate, give one big spring of a leap over the gate and was gone in a flash. Only this time she headed the half a mile back home. We too had a five-foot-plus tall door-type gate, but she scaled this with ease with the aid of the dustbin next to it. My mother had heard a rattle, and the next thing there was Ally at the back door barking to be let in. Liz was not far behind and was grateful that she knew her way home safely. This little episode happened the same time most mornings, and once she had checked every room of the house and saw everything was in order, she went off quite happily with Liz

Slowly I got more confident about not having to tie her on long leashes. Also, like my other dogs, Ally sussed out all the best calls. I have mentioned before that I talked to all my dogs and often told them what was on the day's agenda, thinking that they may not understand but I think they all understood me perfectly. I don't know how Ally knew, but when we got near to one of her favourite stables where she got spoilt rotten with biscuits and fuss, she would cause a commotion in the van. Nothing nasty, just squeaking and yelps with a tail wagging at a hundred miles an hour. It didn't matter which route we took; she knew exactly where we were going.

Ally, too, turned into one of the most faithful and trusting dogs and I suppose my best friend at a very difficult time in my life. Yes, she did have a vice or two which she kept for most of her life, and one was not to let other dogs into our garden or house even invited. The one exception was Ben, a three-year-old Saluki who belonged to Phyl, who eventually became my wife. I met her four years after getting divorced from Judy. Ben was a timid Saluki and very wary of men. It took me a little time to win his trust. The first time I took both dogs for a walk, I had to catch him in a rugby tackle just to put his lead on. Eventually he did trust me, and there was never a problem when it was walkies time. The strange thing was, Ally just accepted him and he took to Ally. It was as if she thought, *Well, he's with her, you'll have to be with me, Ben.* I can remember leaving them both in my nearly new car on their second meeting and expecting the worst when we returned. What happened? Nothing. Both of them just sitting on the back seat, waiting patiently for us. I think they were good for each other. Ally, when with Ben, calmed down and she gave him more confidence not to be so timid.

Ben liked to sit in his favourite fiddleback chair in our kitchen, where he could look out of the window and watch the world go by. If anyone ever came into our yard, he would make a funny bark as if to say to Ally, *I'll spot them; you get them.*

Yes, Benny was just a good lookout, although we found he had a very good weapon for protection of others. Speed. We found this when visiting a country fair. I was with Ally and we were walking in front of Phyl and Ben when a vicious looking dog broke free from its owner and was running and snarling at Ally. Ben saw this, and he too broke free from Phyl and ran at breakneck speed at the not-so-friendly animal. When he made contact at what looked like 100 miles an hour, he sent the brute flying. When the thing was picking itself up off the ground, he was on the way back and over it went again. Luckily the owner by now was on hand to control his dog. He may have come off second best in a fight but not many dogs could match him on speed.

Ally, even though she had her pain in the neck moments, was never slow to show her affection not just to me but many folk. I found this out one day while shoeing for a husband and wife I will call Stella and Steve. Their property consisted of their four-bedroom house, stables for four horses plus a bungalow built in their huge garden for Steve's elderly mother. Thinking that my dog would never escape with a tall brick wall surrounding the property, I never noticed her missing until I was ready to leave. After searching the surrounding area and no dog in sight, a few swear words started to leave my mouth. Then Stella shouts for me to come. She was outside her mother-in-law's bungalow and told me to go in. With my heart pounding ten to the dozen, I was thinking, what mischief has she got up to? I thought Ally had got into her home and done something dreadful and what I saw – was I relieved. There's Ally on the old gal's bed, curled up, with both of them having an afternoon nap, with the mother cuddling up to her.

I didn't know whether to be cross or pleased with her until Stella said, 'Oh, Mick, how lovely, more than likely mother's encouraged her.'

'Knowing my dog, she wouldn't have needed much encouragement,' came my reply.

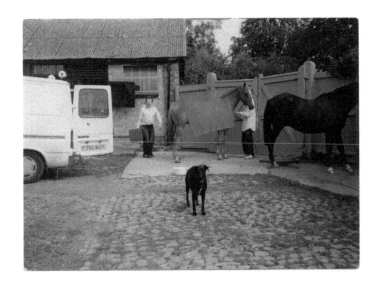

Ally and Ben

MILLENNIUM

When Phyl and I got married on 17 April 1999, Andy was my best man, and the reception was held in a Loughborough hotel. One of my clients, Maggie, a professional singer, did us proud with the evening entertainment. With both of us coming from large families, we found a hotel which had a big function room to cater our needs. It wasn't just family but folk from Phyl's work and many of my clients and fellow farriers. A few days later, we had a honeymoon in the Canary Isles. It was at our wedding, one of my sisters Sheila and her husband, John, and their sons Ben and Tim said they planned to spend the Millennium in Cyprus and would we like to join them. John worked for British Aerospace in Saudi Arabia and didn't fancy seeing the New Year in there.

Both Phyl and I had been to Cyprus before but never with each other. We agreed we both loved the place the last time we were there and we would meet up with John and Sheila. My two sons Chris and Nick came too, and we joined my sister's family in Cyprus. John knew someone who had a couple of apartments and arranged for us to rent them.

It was while we were in Cyprus that I said to Phyl, 'Do you know, I could one day live here.'

'Really so could I,' came her reply.

So 11 months later in November 2000, we went back to Cyprus, house-hunting. Our idea was to use it as a holiday home until the day of our retirement. Well that was our idea. Although we did look at several properties, there was one we really liked. The lady who was selling said her solicitor was on holiday and doubted if anything would get done before Christmas. We thought there would be no rush and gave us time to think we were doing the right thing, so we waited until after Christmas to make an offer. That was a mistake as another party were also interested and must have started the proceedings of buying before Christmas. We thought perhaps we were making a rash decision and it was not meant to happen. If we did make a life in Cyprus, we decided it may be better to rent first.

In March 2002, we had another holiday in Cyprus, and Nick my youngest son was with us. He was interested to see the house we nearly bought 18 months previously. It was on a little private cul-de-sac in a village of Chlorakas on the outskirts of Paphos. While driving past, I noticed anther property was up for sale. I never said anything to Phyl or Nick as we had got it into our heads we were going to rent.

On this holiday, we had got to know Kyriakos who owned a tavern at Coral Bay. He told me his name meant 'the day of the Lord'. It took me a while to remember Kyriakos so we nicknamed him 'The Sunday Man'. We had visited his establishment several times when we mentioned to him one day we wanted to retire to Cyprus. We told him we would rent first before buying when he advised us to buy now as property prices were rising fast.

By the last day of our holiday, we hadn't said a word to each other about buying but on the way to the airport with an hour to kill, I said, 'Let's have one last drive past the house we nearly bought.'

I still hadn't said a word to Phyl or Nick that I noticed another house for sale on the same little complex when we first showed Nick. It turned out they had spotted it too but like me said nothing as we had got it into our heads it's best to rent. This time, though, I stopped outside as I noticed it was a three-bedroom whereas the others were two. I don't know what made me stop, but Phyl said, 'Well, are you going to knock on the door and ask?'

Six weeks later we were on the way back to Cyprus to complete the sale. I found out later what the sellers, Ian and Ann, said about us when I knocked on the door that afternoon. When they saw our hired Suzuki jeep parked outside with suitcases stacked inside, they thought we were tourists on our way home, and Ann had said to Ian, 'Tell them to piss off. Blooming tourists. They just want to have a nose before they catch their flight home.'

The next two years, our retirement home got used many times, not just by us but family and friends. One time while Phyl and I were having a break in Cyprus, Andy Speck and his wife Jackie were on the Island too. We were keen to show off our new home and invited them to visit us. While we were having a beer, enjoying the warm sunny weather sat on the balcony overlooking the sea, Andy and I started to reminisce about old times. I don't think either of us could have dreamt of what we both had achieved. We both remembered the first day we set out in business when we wondered if we could afford food for our dinner. Or worse was the bank manager's lecture going to come true as he doubted we would succeed. Well, that was 35 years ago then, and now, while pouring another beer, we couldn't help but bring up the bank manager's lecture again. We looked back at all the obstacles we had to overcome to succeed.

As for the bank manager having no faith in us, Andy raised his glass to give a toast and said, 'I wonder what that manager is doing now?'

Some folk have said we were lucky to be able to afford what we had got. All I say to these people, luck had got nothing to do with it, but blooming hard work did. If anybody called me lucky for what I had achieved, I would say what stopped them doing the same? Did they leave their house at five thirty in the morning for work and still be at it gone eight in the evening? I would say that wasn't luck but hard graft. Phyl was the same, she very rarely left for home at knocking-off time at five o'clock. Sometimes it would be nearer eight o'clock when she got home.

Two years later (2004) things had changed in our life health-wise. Phyl was struggling with an underactive thyroid. She was always feeling tired, and although her job as an accountant was not physical, it was mentally demanding. With me, I seemed to be suffering all the time with bronchitis and got out of breath easily. We noticed when we went to our holiday home in winter, our health improved with the warmer climate. In February 2004 after one short break, we came back from Cyprus refreshed. Within a week back at work, another chesty cough started which turned into bronchitis. Although I never stopped working, I was starting to get slower at shoeing the horses the way I felt. I knew Phyl was struggling with her problem, and that was when we decided we didn't want to be the richest folk in the graveyard. We knew if I sold our home in the UK, I could afford to retire at 56, hoping the warmer climate would help our health. We had no mortgage to worry about when we sold our house and forge seven months later and moved to Cyprus with our two dogs Ally and Ben.

Before we left, we wanted to say farewell to my clients, fellow farriers, Phyl's work colleagues, friends and family, and booked the function room at the local working men's club.

None of my achievements ever dawned on me until our leaving party. With so many talented farriers in Leicestershire, I had classed work as a competition. None of us could afford to let our standards drop. If that happened, the horse owners would just find someone who could do the job better. Of course, there were the odd cases where one would bang the horse's shoes on cheap, it happens in any job. With me, I never paid too much attention to what any of the other farriers got up to. I concentrated on my own work and let my work do the talking. That is not to say if another farrier had a problem and asked for my help, I would only be only too happy to oblige. I only wanted a good name for us farriers.

I hope I got the trust of lots of younger farriers I had helped over the years. I know lots of the older farriers who held high and important positions in the Farriers Association and other committees welcomed me with open arms. At farrier meetings or other horsey dos, my wife was sure more horses got shod with us farriers talking how best to go about farrier problems. One guy could have had a predicament with something that was not straightforward farrier-wise. It could be anything from a lame horse or the bad condition of a horse's hooves. Whoever was having the problem, you would hear others saying, 'Well, have you tried this, or what about doing that?' The guy that was having the problem knew none of us was trying to belittle him and listened to any ideas. Next time, it may be him having a good idea about another matter. Looking back now, I can see Phyl's point of view, we did get through an awful lot of horseshoeing at the many banqueting functions that our wives must have found boring. (I mean us farriers talking of horseshoeing not the banquet.)

It never entered my head that one day I would be voted to become chairman of the Leicester Branch of farriers. Life then started to get hectic in a nice way. Attending boardroom meetings at the farrier's headquarters at Stoneleigh showground. (The Royal Showground.) AGMs hosted by different county branches every year. One year it was Pitlochry in Scotland, the next year it was Bournemouth on the south coast. I liked to think I gave my tuppence ha'penny worth of suggestions at those meetings. Sometimes, disagreements were often ironed out in lively debates, but all in all, it was to make farriery standards better.

Two or three years after I became chairman of the Leicester branch, I was elected chairman of all the East Midlands branches (The District) after one AGM too. Again all eyes seemed to look in my direction when the last chairman resigned. One person put my name forward, and God knows how many more wanted to second it. Mind you, the others had probably thought Mick's in the room; let's vote for him.

Being chairman of two branches did become hectic, and after two years I decided that one role had to go. So I resigned as chairman of the Leicestershire branch and concentrated on the East Midlands until I retired in 2004.

I was also on the farrier's craft committee. The craft committee organised lectures and demonstrations, not just for apprentices but also for qualified farriers too. These meetings could be on techniques on anything from how to work the anvil and hold a hammer or to describe the finer points in surgical horseshoe making for different lameness, etcetera. Sometimes vets gave a lecture on various types of lameness in horses or talks on what feed is good for a horse and what's bad. There were loads of topics, technology was always moving forward, and there was never a shortage of people to talk about them.

I was also the auditor for the Farriers Association for a couple of years before I retired. It meant spending a day at Stoneleigh, our association head office, checking the association books once a year that everything was in order. The biggest thrill about getting that job was at that one particular AGM, out of sixty-odd delegates, sixty-odd were in favour of me. Mind you, I got the feeling no one else wanted the job.

Regardless of whether others did or didn't want these positions, I still feel highly honoured to be asked. I think it wasn't until we were having our leaving do that I realised how much other farriers and horse owners thought of me. Phyl and I thought we might get around 50 guests and that included family, but more than double that turned up. My brother's (Kev) band Wellard Willy (named after dogs in *EastEnders*, so I am told) supplied the evening's entertainment.

I got a little bit overwhelmed that night. Clients, some I had done work for many years, started to stand up and to give their speeches on the various problems their horses had and what I had done to cure them. Caroline Cotton was one of the many clients who stood up and said how John (the vet) and I saved her best dressage horse's life. She also admitted that she had expected the worst and was surprised John and I and never once said it was a hopeless case.

I replied, 'You were expecting the worst, so were we, but we didn't dare tell you,' to everybody's amusement.

I listened and felt a little big-headed from all those wonderful people saying good things about me; now it was my turn to thank everybody who had turned up that night. Feeling emotional about what to say after saying thank you a million times, I was becoming stuck on what else to say when I saw a couple of ladies accompanied with their teenage daughters. I had shod their horses and ponies since they were thirteen-year-old kids themselves. I had to remind them about when Willy and I caught them trying to have a crafty fag when they were kids at the gymkhana organised by the Leicestershire farriers. The two had just lit a cigarette and only took one puff when a look of horror appeared on their faces, and they threw the unfinished smoked fags to the ground well away from them. At the same time, wafting their hands in front of their faces, trying to hide the cigarette smoke. Willy knew what was happening when he saw a man walking briskly towards us.

He picked the discarded lit cigarettes up and shouted, 'Hey, girls, look. You have thrown new fags away, who do you say is coming, your dad? Doesn't he know you smoke?'

Their faces were a picture. It was also a picture that night, too, not only for me reminding them. It was the lecture off one of their daughters, disgusted they were smoking at 13.

When I thought the speeches had come to an end, Mick Woodford, a respected farrier who is a dedicated guy the profession is lucky to have, had to jump on stage with a package under his arm. He had been asked to award me a certificate on behalf of the Farrier Association for my services to the profession. Again, I was not expecting anything like that and again stuck for words apart from repeating myself with thank you a million times, and never in my wildest dreams was I expecting this. Oh, what a send-off, and the evening finished with guests singing along to 'Delilah' that Kev's band were preforming.

Horse needs attention on Leicestershire county showground.

Danny boy meets Desert Orchid.

Dave Gulley presenting me with a decanter.

Stuart Spence presenting me with a bottle
of whisky to fill the decanter.

Mick Woodford admiring my present.

A week or so before we departed for Cyprus, I attended my last Leicester Farriers branch meeting. Once all the business on the agenda was dealt with, the attention turned to me with 10 or so farriers who wanted to wish me well. Some I had worked with and others we shared advice with over the years. I felt privileged to have got into a profession where a group of guys could be so competitive in a nice way. I was asked by the new chairman Richard Spence if it was OK for him to have a trophy inscribed with Mick and Phyl O'Reardon on it to be awarded at the branch's farrier competition. We were only too happy to have an award presented in our honour.

Again at this meeting, I was not expecting to be saying thank you so many times. I was stuck for what to say with all the kind words these guys had to say about me. Dave Gulley presented me with a lovely decanter inscribed with the Leicestershire Farriers branch and my name on it. That still sits proudly in our glasses cabinet to this day.

When we finally left for Cyprus on 22 September 2004, I had shod my last horse, and Phyl had done her last accounts. Well, that's what we thought!

Lightning Source UK Ltd.
Milton Keynes UK
UKHW021326171221
395752UK00006B/137

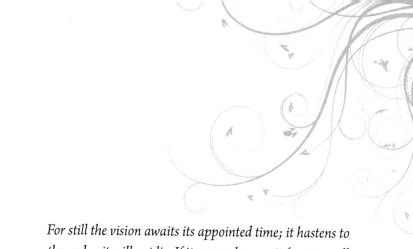

For still the vision awaits its appointed time; it hastens to the end—it will not lie. If it seems slow, wait for it; it will surely come; it will not delay.

Habakkuk 2:3

CPSIA information can be obtained
at www.ICGtesting.com
Printed in the USA
BVHW040753110821
614095BV00027BA/427

9 781953 156273